WHAT IS HYPNOSIS?

What Every Person Should Know About Hypnosis

Drake Eastburn

For information, contact Eastburn Hypnotherapy Center
7905 N. Zenobia St.
Westminster, CO 80030
303-424-2331
office@hypnodenver.com

The author of this book does not—either directly or indirectly—dispense medical advice or prescribe the use of any technique as a form of treatment for physical, emotional, or medical problems without the advice of a physician. The intent of the author is only to offer information of a general nature to help you in your quest for weight mastery as well as for physical, mental and emotional wellbeing. The author and publisher assume no responsibility for your actions in regards to your use (or non-use) of the information in this book. No promises or guarantees are made—express or implied.

Order this book online at www.trafford.com
or email orders@trafford.com

Most Trafford titles are also available at major online book retailers.

Printed in the United States of America.

ISBN: 978-1-4269-4036-1 (sc)

Trafford rev. 12/30/2010

 www.trafford.com

North America & international
toll-free: 1 888 232 4444 (USA & Canada)
phone: 250 383 6864 ♦ fax: 812 355 4082

Also by Drake Eastburn

The Power of Suggestion
(2010)

No Time to Waist—Powerful Hypnotic Weight Loss Secrets You <u>NEED</u> To Know
(2010)

Power Patter
(2008)

The Power of the Past
(2007)

TABLE OF CONTENTS

DEDICATION

This book is dedicated to all of the hypnotists who have ever found themselves trying to defend and/or define hypnosis to some misguided, fearful individual who simply doesn't understand what hypnotism actually is. And also to those members of society who would benefit from a clearer comprehension of hypnosis. It is my hope that through better overall understanding of hypnotism we will alleviate or even eliminate those fears and unwarranted beliefs, and the general public will become more inclined to participate in, and benefit from, the use of hypnosis.

ACKNOWLEDGMENTS

There are many people and organizations that deserve my thanks. My first formal introduction to hypnosis was in the early seventies with the *Silva Method*. The late Jose Silva created a hypnosis training (although he avoided using the term hypnosis) that has been embraced by many over the years. The *Silva Method* has been the introduction into the world of hypnosis for a lot of people.

I became involved in the *Silva Method* out of my own desire for personal growth. The *Silva Method* was a great place to start. It focused on positive thinking and positive mental attitude. Today the movie *The Secret* has become very popular; however, the *Silva Method* had a similar focus many years before *The Secret* came along.

I came from a very dysfunctional and negative thinking family environment. I did very poorly in school and was not likely to become the kind of person who would excel in life at all. But through Silva I learned that simply by changing my thoughts, I could change my life. I am here to say that this is absolutely so.

Even though Jose Silva passed away some ten years ago, I believe trainings and advanced *Silva Method* classes are still taking place. Silva's youngest daughter, Laura, is a very dynamic speaker and teacher in her own right and I believe she is still active in the field.

In those days (the seventies) I was suffering from migraines and I learned the techniques of Silva to control those migraines. I can honestly say I have not experienced another migraine since the 1970s, and I have certainly helped many others to achieve that freedom as well.

I have to thank my good friends Patrick Shirk and the late Jerry Haskins. We all became friends in a hypnosis class that Pat was teaching through a local university. We joined forces and went into business together, applying hypnosis principles to create wealth. Jerry died in an automobile accident some time ago, but he would probably be the most excited of any of us about how far the use of hypnosis has progressed.

I met my wife, Lynsi, nine years ago at a National Guild of Hypnotists convention in New Hampshire. Her influence in the area of hypnosis has had a profound effect on the work I do today. Her expertise in the area of hypnosis for fertility, the classes she teaches in this area of hypnosis, and her book *It's Conceivable!* are major contributions to the world of hypnosis today.

A special thanks goes out to the National Guild of Hypnotists (NGH). The NGH is the largest and most prestigious organization of its kind in the field of hypnosis. There are other similar organizations and I have belonged to them and taught for them; however, NGH has the highest standards. The Guild is the only body of its type that has a standardized training, promotes a standard of ethics and practice that is the model in our field, and provides a union and many other benefits for the professional hypnotist. There are many individuals out there who are doing great work in the field of hypnosis and they deserve to be recognized for their achievements and those achievements need to be brought to the attention of those who could benefit from them. However, if those individuals are not involved in an organization like the NGH then they will go unrecognized and the benefit that could be passed on to others will be missed.

Sometimes we can take organizations for granted whether they are companies, governments or those such as the Guild. People find it easy to complain about these organizations at times; however, the more I am involved with the Guild, and the more I get to know the people who run NGH, the more impressed I am with what they have provided to the community of hypnosis. Dwight Damon and his family are the main influence supported by a board of professionals and volunteers who help in many ways such as conducting classes for the Guild.

The Guild conventions are the finest in the industry and we hypnotists are the beneficiaries of their efforts. The work that the National Guild of Hypnotists has done may be the single biggest contribution to the modern world of hypnosis.

A big thanks goes to Jerry Kein and Omni Hypnosis. Jerry has trained more people in the use of hypnosis than we could ever know. One of the things I like the most about Jerry is that he does hypnosis. His hypnosis isn't watered down or fluffed up with something else, it's the real deal. Jerry has been so generous to allow me to use his famous mind model, which has become a very useful tool for me. Find more about Jerry in the reference section.

Special thanks go out to my good friends Martie O'Brien and Anita Distephano who have done such a good job of faithfully editing and typesetting my books. My lovely wife, Lynsi, is the master of editing, as well as typesetting, and she has so graciously given her valuable time to this project.

What is Hypnosis? Sponsors

Aniela Johnson
A Higher Alignment
Denver, CO
303-519-6258
www.ahigheralignment.com

Aniela Johnson CH is a Clinical Hypnotherapist from the Eastburn Hypnotherapy Institute of Denver. She graduated from Metro State College with a degree in Behavioral Science and with a minor in education. Aniela has received extensive training in hypnotherapy, as well as specialty certifications in Birth by Hypnosis™, HypnoFertility˚, Pain Management, Past Life and Age Regression, Weight Management, Anxiety, and Smoking Cessation. Aniela is a member of the National Guild of Hypnotists. She has a special interest in helping people develop a mind/body connection through hypnosis.

Stacey Horn, LCSW, CH
Family Room CO, Inc.
PO Box 6042
Eagle CO. 81631-6042
Telephone 970-688-1401
www.familyroomco.net
Offices in Avon and Eagle

Stacey has been a Solution Focused Clinical Social Worker for 21 years, specializing in Substance Abuse and Mental Health issues. Stacey was born with Hypnosis, and 45 years later used HypnoBirthing® to birth her daughter Moria! She completed her Hypnosis training with Eastburn Hypnotherapy Center, which has been an excellent tool in her practice. Her specialties include Women's Issues, Smoking Cessation and pain management with or without medications and *Loves Nothing More Than A Challenge!*

Karen L Riley, BSc, PDCHyp, D.Hyp, HBCE, HFT, MBSCH
Registered Clinical Hypnotherapist
UK Director - HypnoFertility Foundation

Clinical Hypnosis in Huddersfield, Halifax, West Yorkshire, Yorkshire, UK
01484 485380
01422 373321
Mobile 07966 968367
E-Mail: smiley.rileys@virgin.net
http://karenriley-hypnotherapy.com

Karen Riley is a leading clinical hypnotist and hypnotherapist based in Huddersfield, West Yorkshire. She has an academic background in human biology and has extensive training and experience in Clinical Hypnosis, Hypnotherapy, Hypno-analysis, Suggestion therapy and EMDR.

She is a full member of the prestigious British Society of Clinical Hypnosis, a fellow of the NLPPA, the UK Director of the HypnoFertility Foundation, a tutor for the London College of Clinical Hypnosis and a member of the Complementary Therapy Research Network. Karen is also an accredited trainer of hypnosis and teaches GP's, medical consultants, midwives and nurses about hypnosis and hypnotherapy.

Karen successfully works with people from all over the UK, with a wide range of issues at her clinic based in Huddersfield, where she specialises in anxiety based issues, irritable bowel syndrome, fertility and childbirth. Karen can regularly be seen as the hypnotherapy expert in national women's and health magazines, has made contributions to published books on hypnosis and hypnofertility. Karen is the creator of the internationally selling fertility and conception hypnosis programme.

Robert Riddlemoser
Phone: 303-623-2003
Cell: 720-256-0762
email: rcfraia@gmail.com

Loving Learning. As a child you loved to learn, you loved it so much you could not stop asking questions. "Mommy, why is the sky blue," and on and on. Something happened and most of us misplaced the burning desire to learn. But, the desire can be accessed and anchored with hypnosis. Yes, you can love learning just as much as you did as a kid.

The techniques employed are the full range of hypnotherapy including stress reduction, regression to childhood to recover the joy and love of learning, resolution of past trauma, motivation enhancement and organizing for success.

Robert comes from a technical professional background, augmented by teaching and therapeutic experience and training. He is a licensed architect and has worked as an engineer and a construction manager. As such he gets right to the point, enabling the client to learn the information, the techniques and the problem solving abilities, and thus bypassing pointless ritual that never worked.

He specializes in rapid learning in Professional Continuing Education, Math, Science, overcoming learning disabilities, easing test anxiety, improving study skills and new language acquisition.

Tracy Jones, BA(Hons), MSc, ACMA, DipCAH, HPD, MNCH(Lic)

Company name: Cariad Hypnotherapy
Locations: Wrexham & Chester, UK
Telephone: +44 1978 363629
Website: www.cariadhypnotherapy.co.uk
Email: tracy@cariadhypnotherapy.co.uk

Tracy is a registered Clinical Hypnotherapist, Certified HypnoBirthing˙ Practitioner and HypnoFertility˙ Therapist. She has busy practices in North Wales and Chester in the UK, working with individuals and couples with an aim to empower them to make positive changes in their lives. Whilst specialising in hypnosis for fertility, childbirth and parenting, she also works with clients on lifestyle changes such as weight loss & eating habits, smoking cessation, anxiety & stress management, self esteem, confidence and performance coaching.

Tatiana Korol & Michael Smith
847.760.5000
www.TrainingInHypnotherapy.com

Tatiana and Michael are the owners of the AlternativePractitionerAcademy.com – An Illinois state licensed school providing training in fundamental and advanced hypnotism for over 10 years. Among students, their school has earned a reputation of being "the only place you can trust to provide adequate information from the best teachers". On the other hand, experts in the field like Lynsi Eastburn, Roy Hunter or Ron Eslinger have "consistently found APA (The Alternative Practitioner Academy) graduates to be knowledgeable, proficient and professional hypnotherapists".

Tatiana and Michael are certified in Clinical & Medical Hypnotism and members of the National Guild of Hypnotists. They are also certified HypnoBirthing˚ Fertility Therapists. Michael Smith is specializing in trauma resolutions as well as fears and phobias. Tatiana's passion is in the area of physical issues like unexplained infertility, endometriosis or cysts. Her unique and effective Transpersonal Transformation method, which she is teaching now to other certified hypnotists, has also helped people with skin issues like psoriasis, blood issues like high cholesterol, blood sugar or blood clots to achieve profound results that in some cases were identified by doctors as "miraculous healing".

FOREWORD

Are you in hypnosis? Right now? Do you remember being in trance yesterday? (You will soon know why I am asking this question.)

For that matter, what *is* hypnosis? As director of the National Guild of Hypnotists International Annual Convention, I am asked that question at least once a week as I travel. And, thankfully, Drake Eastburn has come to the rescue with this long-needed expanded explanation of hypnosis in such a way that you will emerge with a far better understanding.

Drake is an engaging guide as we tour through the history of earlier attempts at "explaining" hypnosis, and then helps us get clear on the truest of meanings.

Drake discovered, early in his life, the power of hypnosis to bring about positive change, and then shared this knowledge with thousands of clients with what can only be called historic success.

As you embark on this journey with Drake, two things are about to happen: your passion for hypnosis is going to be stronger than ever, as will your curiosity for further exploration . . . both traits of a great book.

—Elsom Eldridge Jr.
Author of ***The Obvious Expert***

INTRODUCTION

I have been contemplating writing a book called *What Is Hypnosis* for several years. I feel that what most people believe hypnosis to be is either partially correct or completely off base. Even many hypnotists don't seem to truly understand what hypnosis is.

One day I was in a used book store and came across a small paperback entitled *What Is Hypnosis*. This book was written by Andrew Salter and was first published in 1941. When I saw this book I thought to myself, well, here it is, I won't need to write that book after all. I paid a dollar for the book and discovered it was focused mainly on conditioned response (Pavlovian response) and didn't actually explain hypnosis beyond conditioned response.

In this book, I will give some of the common definitions of hypnosis and will explain the accuracies and inaccuracies of those definitions. Within this text I will attempt to give the much broader picture of what I believe hypnosis to be.

At the end of this book you will find a large glossary of related hypnosis terms. I have tried to keep it fairly mainstream and, hopefully, easy to understand. I believe that when we have a good understanding of the terminology that is associated with any subject we will then have a much better understanding of that subject in general.

I believe that everyone would benefit from a better understanding of hypnosis. Too many people believe hypnosis involves some sort of mind control or brain washing which creates an immediate sense of fear. But they would be much more inclined to seek out help from their local hypnotist if they had a better understanding of what hypnosis actually is.

The truth is, whether people realize it or not, hypnosis (trance) is a part of our normal, daily lives. I tend to use the terms "hypnosis" and "trance" interchangeably and I think we would all do well to embrace that terminology. Hypnosis is our friend if we take advantage of it.

IF YOU THINK YOU HAVEN'T BEEN HYPNOTIZED . . .

"There isn't a person alive of normal intelligence and over the age of two who has not been hypnotized, and if you are in your later years, you have been hypnotized many times. If you doubt this, you don't know what hypnosis is."

—Dave Elman
Hypnotherapy, p. 17

Chapter 1

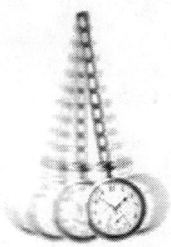

COMMON DEFINITIONS OF HYPNOSIS

Definition by Gil Boyne, the president of The American Counsel of Hypnotist Examiners:

An extraordinary quality of mental, physical, and emotional relaxation.

An emotionalized desire to satisfy the hypnotist's instructions, directions, and suggestions, except with those that generate conflict with the subject's values, i.e. character, attitudes, religious beliefs, and moral principals.

The organism becomes self-regulating as the trance produces normalization of the central nervous system.

Heightened and selective sensitivity to stimuli perceived by the five senses and the basic perception.

Immediate softening of psychic defenses.

Lack of response to irrelevant, external stimuli.

Operating theory is that electro biochemical changes take place in the nervous system as a result of the brain being stimulated by words and images.

Andre M. Weitzenhoffer:

Hypnosis is a condition or state of selective hyper suggestibility brought about in an individual (subject) through the use of certain specific psychological or physical manipulation of this individual by another person (hypnotist).

Definition by Rev. Dr. C. Scot Giles, Head of the NGH Ethics Committee:

During hypnotic trance, a change occurs in the structure of the brain where the two halves are linked. Because of this change, more information flows from one side of the brain to the other than would normally be the case.

Nerve cells in the part of the brain that controls habit lose some of their electrical charge enabling one to become more receptive to change at this time. Through imagery and positive suggestion, new connections can be formed among the nerve cells, creating the desired results.

Definition from Wikipedia:

Hypnosis (from the Greek hypnos, "sleep") is often thought to be "a trance-like state that resembles sleep but is induced by a person whose suggestions are readily accepted by the subject." However, this is disputed and there is a great deal of evidence to indicate that the behaviors, experiences, and phenomena associated with hypnosis are in fact variations of everyday experiences.

Definition by Jerry Kein of Omni Hypnosis:

Hypnosis is the bypass of the critical factor of the conscious mind and the establishment of selective thinking.

This is very similar to the definition used by Dave Elman. Elman also stated that hypnosis is not a condition but a state.

Definition from Hypnotism 1945 by Axel Wayne Bacon:

Hypnosis is merely a case of exaggerated suggestibility, brought about by the hypnotist. In this state the subject is highly cooperative.

Definition from Practical Lessons in Hypnotism 1943, By WM. Wesley Cook, A.M., M.D. Professor of Physiological Medicine in the National University of Chicago:

Hypnotism is the science and art of mentally controlling the thoughts and actions of others. Its study embraces a knowledge of the methods best adapted for developing personal mental power and directing the mental activities of others.

Definition by Lee Rindner:

Any subconscious response is hypnosis.

Definition by Masud Ansari, PhD, from his book Modern Hypnosis:

Modern Hypnosis: Due to the polymorphous nature of hypnosis and the disagreements among hypnotist scholars about its reality, there is no consensus or definition.

Ansari went on to quote Cooke and Vogt who state:

Present day knowledge of hypnosis might roughly be translated to the knowledge of electricity half a century ago. The electron was undiscovered and so it was impossible to define electricity as a flow of electrons through a conducting material. And yet, though no definition was possible, a mighty science and a mighty industry were growing and new uses for electricity were discovered daily. It might be said, therefore, that some as yet undiscovered psychological or physiological (electron) may give us, in time, a theory of hypnosis which will account for all of the observed phenomena. At present we must be content to say we don't know what it is, but we are beginning to understand how it works.

Ansari finds it necessary to give it a working definition as follows: "Hypnosis is a particular altered state of selective hyper suggestibility brought about in an individual by the use of a combination of relaxation, fixation or attention, and suggestion."

Definition by Ernest R. Hilgard:

In his in depth study of hypnosis *The Experience of Hypnosis* Ernest R. Hilgard in the chapter *What is Hypnosis* states, "Hypnosis resists precise definition."

Chapter 2

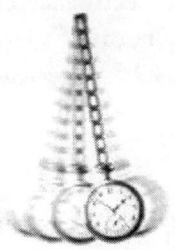

WHAT IS HYPNOSIS?

While each of the definitions in the previous chapter has some truth to it, do any of them completely describe what hypnosis is? If hypnosis was a chair, it would be easy for me to just pull out a chair, point to it and say, "This is hypnosis." Even though some chairs (hypnosis) take a somewhat different form, they are all fairly easy to identify. The problem is that in reality the many faces of hypnosis vary widely. Hypnosis is not something tangible like a chair that we can visually inspect to determine what it is. Because of this the definition of hypnosis becomes more ambiguous.

William James (Neophytou, 1996):
> Our normal waking consciousness is but one special type of consciousness, whilst all about if by the flimsiest screens, there lie potential forms of consciousness entirely different . . . No account

of the universe in its totality can be final, which leaves these other forms of consciousness quite disregarded.

In my world there is nothing but hypnosis (trance); it's just a matter of what state of hypnosis (trance) we may be in at any given moment. In order to have a definition of hypnosis we would also need to know exactly what hypnosis isn't. We could then say that "normal waking consciousness" is not hypnosis. I could agree with that, however I believe that the term "normal waking consciousness" is also rather ambiguous.

Beta is the level of consciousness that we refer to as normal waking consciousness. Beta occurs from between 14-21 CPS (cycles per second of brain waves, measured by an electroencephalograph machine). The beta level is where we experience "normal" physical activity. However, is the person who is generating 14 CPS experiencing the world the same as a person at the same time and place who is generating 21 CPS?

When I talk about this in any of my classes and everyone in the room is listening to what I am saying, we might assume that everyone falls within that same 14-21 CPS area and so everyone could be assumed to be in a beta state. However, there are completely different experiences going on in the room at the same time. While one person may be totally fixated and intellectualizing my every word, some other student is about to fall asleep. Another student is dreaming about sitting on a tropical beach with that attractive student in the seat in front of them. Someone else is wondering about their bank statement or when is this class going to end. Someone else is hoping that I will just shut up and move on to something else. All of these different experiences are occurring at the same time and yet we assume that these people are all having a beta experience of the world.

But are they? Can we assume that all of these individuals are actually falling within that 14-21 CPS range? Both things are likely to be true. I doubt that we stay within any given range of consciousness (14-21 CPS) for long. And even within that range of consciousness we could be having very different kinds of experiences. So you can see what we think of as "normal waking consciousness" is an enigmatic thing. Even if we could monitor our brain waves constantly there would not necessarily be any indication of whether we were in hypnosis at any given moment. I believe that all states of consciousness are hypnosis; it's more a matter of what *state* of hypnosis (trance) we are in at any given moment.

Dr. James Braid is considered by most hypnotists to be the father of modern hypnosis. He is given that distinction mainly because he is the one who coined the term "hypnosis," a Greek word for "sleep." However hypnosis is not sleep (or maybe not). Once Braid realized that the term hypnosis was not accurate, he tried to change it, but the term had already taken hold and it stuck.

When hypnosis is defined as an extremely or profoundly relaxed state, that statement can be true in some situations. Certainly as hypnotists we use the word *relax* (and all of its variations) frequently, and many times relaxed is what we are going for. But isn't the person in a stage hypnosis show who is running around and yelling out absurdities also hypnotized? Of course he *is* hypnotized, just not relaxed. There are many situations where someone is hypnotized but not relaxed. So while saying hypnosis is a state of relaxation might help to get you a passing grade on an exam, it is only partly correct.

If we are actually asleep, then surely we are not hypnotized, right? Yes and no. People who have not experienced hypnosis much may associate it with sleep. The reason this happens is because sometimes sleep is the closest model they have for the hypnosis that they have just experienced. That does not necessarily make the two things the same. Although we normally would not refer to sleep and hypnosis as the same thing, we do use the terms *sleeping hypnosis* or *hypno-sleep* or *hypnosis attached to sleep*. This basically means that we can and do gain hypnotic effects while in a sleep state. I suggest that it is even a good thing to put this hypnotic effect to use. An easy way to do this is through audio recordings. We can give ourselves our own positive suggestions or learn a foreign language while we are asleep at night. Our subconscious is available to use at almost all levels of consciousness, with the possible exception of a deep Delta state.

Some will define hypnosis as a state of heightened suggestibility.* This is true and at some levels of consciousness we are much more suggestible. However we can be very suggestible in any state, which tends to reinforce my feeling that we are always hypnotized. Even in the most conscious waking state we are suggestible. Depending on who is doing the suggesting—and how the suggestion is given—the influence these suggestions will have on us will have varying degrees of success.

If your doctor tells you to quit smoking because you are about to have a coronary, that suggestion may be more successful than if your spouse or a TV ad had given the same suggestion. Likewise, if your drill sergeant gets in your face and demands that you take some sort of action it will have a greater effect than if a friend or family member were to suggest the same thing. Even in this waking state we can achieve what is called *waking hypnosis*, which often means achieving the bypass of the critical faculty (for some this is the definition of hypnosis). I will explain the bypass of the critical faculty later in this chapter.

It is more accurate to say that heightened suggestibility is a condition of being in the state of hypnosis.

The following shows the various levels of consciousness that we often refer to in hypnosis. CPS stands for cycles per second as measured by an electroencephalograph machine.

LEVELS OF CONSCIOUSNESS

Beta
- 14 to 21 CPS
- Considered to be normal waking consciousness or outer world conscious level
- Normal physical action is experienced
- Normal physical world of sight, sound, touch, smell, and taste.

Alpha
- 7-14 CPS
- The beginning of inner consciousness levels
- Self-hypnosis
- Meditation
- E.S.P.
- Increased suggestibility
- Time distortion
- Sleep (including REM sleep) begins

Theta
- 4-7 CPS
- E.S.P.
- Time distortion
- Suggestibility
- Sleep, including REM
- Somnambulism
- Painless surgery and dentistry

Delta
- 4 CPS and below
- Unconscious
- Not great for hypnosis or sleep
- Great for physical healing

Gamma
- Above 21 CPS to about 40 CPS
- State of hyper-alert
- Fight or flight

I have already referred to the beta state as what we consider normal waking consciousness. Now, I will explain about the Alpha state.

Alpha is what we refer to as the beginning of inner consciousness levels. Jose Silva referred to the alpha state as the level of consciousness where we have access to the conscious and the subconscious mind equally. This makes the alpha level ideal for self hypnosis because the conscious mind is present enough to give suggestions, while the subconscious is more receptive to those suggestions. Likewise, meditation occurs at this level. If the meditator is experienced, even deeper levels of consciousness can be achieved.

Time distortion is something hypnotists are familiar with and we certainly can experience this at the alpha level. We have all experienced this distortion at different times. For the young child waiting for Santa Claus to bring that new red bicycle on Christmas morning the time will drag on forever. When the sun starts coming up in the morning at the end of your first big date with Peggy Sue or Billy Joe Bob, it seems like no time at all has gone by before it's over. As a youngster didn't it seem like summer vacation would never come? And then the new school year was upon you before you knew it. Even after a lengthy hypnosis session a client will often report that the session only felt like it took a few minutes. This is a common response. If however the hypnotist suggests that it was a much longer time, then that more lengthy time period is the experience the client is likely to have.

In the *theta* level, time distortion, sleep (including REM) and suggestibility are much more likely. This is the level of consciousness that most hypnotists like to use when giving suggestions to a client, because the subconscious is more accessible and more likely to take the suggestions. This is the state of hypnosis where *somnambulism* occurs. Literally translated, somnambulism means awake and asleep at the same time, and it has come to mean "a deep state of hypnosis." It is in this state of hypnosis that painless surgery and dentistry can be performed.

There is very little brain wave activity at the *delta* level, 4 CPS and below, (but not too much below or we would cease to exist). This level of consciousness is probably the level that we know the least about. It does not seem that we are very receptive to suggestion in this state and while this would seem like a great state for sleep, we actually get better quality sleep in those levels where we are dreaming. Most of the research that is being done with delta level of consciousness is of a medical nature. We do know that this level is good for physical healing.

The gamma level of consciousness is not one that we make much use of as hypnotists. Gamma is that state of consciousness that we achieve after the fourth or fifth cup of coffee of the morning. You might be in a gamma state if you are walking through the deep woods in bear country and hear a branch snap behind you. When your heart is pounding out of your chest and you've gone flush, you might be in a gamma state. Gamma is not a state of consciousness that we would want to spend much time in; it is reserved for those emergency events when we need to respond quickly to save our lives (fight of flight). It would be very stressful to stay in a gamma state for any length of time.

It is likely that we are extremely suggestible while in a gamma state since there is a good chance that we have a total bypass of the critical faculty. We do know that when we have that bypass the subconscious is most accessible for suggestion. The problem is that the gamma state is not a state that lends itself well to study or clinical use. Putting people into a gamma state to see how suggestible they are is not very practical.

It does seem curious to me that in three of the five states of consciousness we have looked at we can be asleep. In two of those three states we can be doing things that would seem very unlike sleep, yet generating the same amount of brainwaves—and actually this is the case. While I talk about sleep elsewhere in this book, sleep seems to occur when there is a total suspension of conscious mind activity. This means, that either thing could be happening while generating the same amount of brainwaves. If we return to the example I gave of all of the students in my classroom having vastly different experiences at the same time, we can begin to understand just how meaningful this is.

One of the definitions of hypnosis I referred to earlier was by Jerry Kein and it has to do with the bypass of the critical factor. Jerry created a mind model that we frequently use to describe how the mind works from a hypnotic standpoint and how the critical faculty becomes formed. I am including that model here (see following page) with an explanation since I will be referring to it from time to time.

The outer circle of the diagram represents the conscious mind. The conscious mind is where intellectual, critical, rational, analytical and judgmental thinking occurs, and where short term memory is stored.

The middle circle represents the subconscious mind. This is the part of the mind that hypnotists are most concerned with. The subconscious houses the creative, imaginative, and emotional components, and long term memory. Habits are also a part of the subconscious mind.

The unconscious mind, for our purposes, incorporates the autonomic nervous system and the immune system. We can and do at times control things like our breathing, heart rate or blood pressure. However, for the most part we don't walk around thinking, "I need to breathe in or pump more blood to the brain." We generally take these things for granted and go about our daily lives.

When we first come into the world our subconscious is wide open to receive information. It needs to be that way because there is so much to take in. All the information that comes in is accepted as truth (regardless of whether it is accurate). This information begins to create a history for us, and the critical factor becomes formed around this information that is being absorbed. Paradigms, or models and beliefs about how the world is supposed to operate, are a part of the critical faculty. The more we receive certain input, the stronger the critical faculty becomes around that input.

Let's say that as a little baby, you play with a toy in a certain way that impresses the adults around you, and they comment on how good that is and how smart you are. As time goes on, more and more of these incidents occur that demonstrate a high level of intelligence (or perceived intelligence), and again the adults continue to comment on your level of intelligence in a positive way. Each time we do something that seems intelligent and it gets reinforced, the critical faculty becomes stronger. Later on, after the critical faculty has been fully formed, any conflicting information that comes in is rejected because it is not consistent with the critical faculty that was created around being intelligent.

What if that information coming in wasn't favorable? What if the information that was given early on is, *that baby takes after its grandmother and you know she was not the sharpest tool in the shed.* That sort of thing might even seem fairly innocuous, but a belief, an expectation is being

Hypnosis and the Mind
Mind Model by Gerald F. Kein

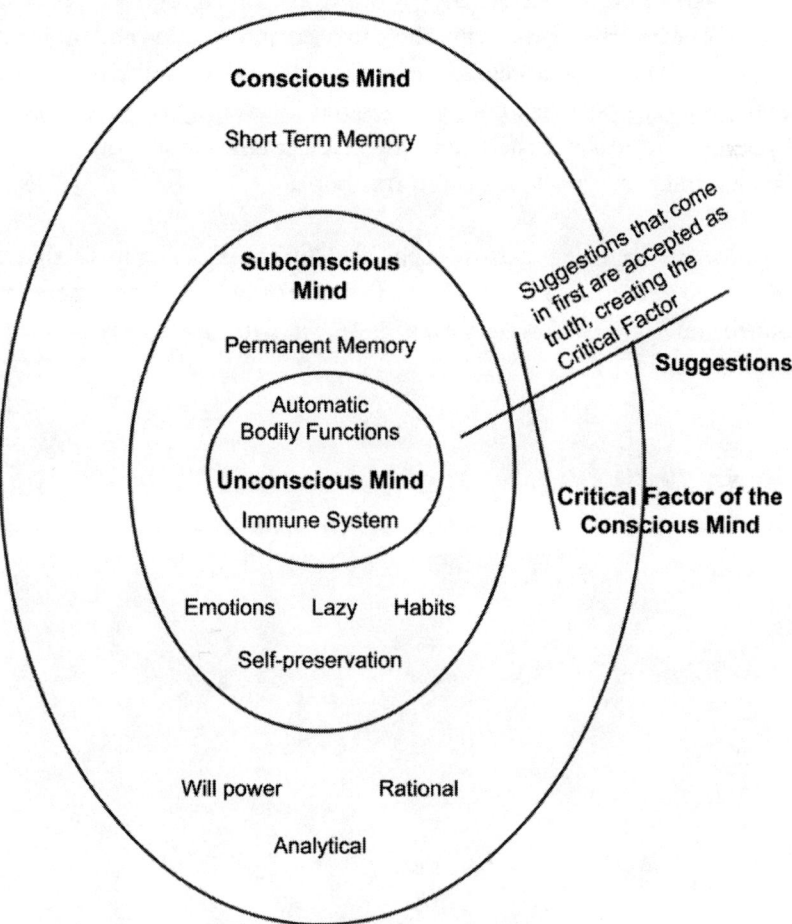

Conscious Mind

Short Term Memory

Subconscious Mind

Permanent Memory

Automatic Bodily Functions

Unconscious Mind

Immune System

Emotions   Lazy   Habits

Self-preservation

Will power   Rational

Analytical

Suggestions that come in first are accepted as truth, creating the Critical Factor

Suggestions

Critical Factor of the Conscious Mind

Hypnosis is the by-pass of the Critical Factor
of the Conscious Mind and the establishment of
acceptable selective thinking.

formed, and little suggestions here and there create a belief (hypnosis) that this kid is not too smart. This also creates an expectation in everyone involved until it is accepted as fact (whether it really is so or not). Now the critical faculty is formed around *I am stupid.* Any information that comes in that would contradict the critical faculty is rejected and that person goes on believing him/herself to be stupid.

When Jerry talks about the bypass of the critical factor, he is referring to moments when that shield is not there to reject information and information (suggestions) will be accepted, much as when we were little babies. This to me is a very pure form of hypnosis and it certainly is <u>one</u> definition of hypnosis, but it is not the whole enchilada. I talk more about the critical faculty and the bypass later on in this book.

So now we have some of the typical definitions of hypnosis that have been used over time. I have raised a few questions about those definitions, but to muddy up the waters even more, we will take a look at what else hypnosis is.

Chapter 3

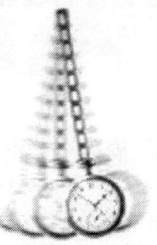

WHAT ELSE IS HYPNOSIS?

Early in my life we lived in an old, rundown duplex in Lincoln, Nebraska. I remember being across the alley from our place, in the backyard at my friend, Drusilla's house. I was lying on my back on the lawn looking up at the sky while watching the cloud formations drift about. To this day I recall experiencing certain sensations that felt really good. I recall feeling very relaxed and feeling as though I were stuck to the lawn and couldn't move. It seemed as though I could have remained there indefinitely just enjoying these comforting sensations.

Looking back, I realize these pleasant sensations I was experiencing were sensations of hypnosis. Certainly at that time I had no idea what an impact on my life these simple sensations would end up having. I must have been no more than three years old at the time, and at three years old we are predominantly generating brainwaves in the delta region, which is to say that we are very much in the subconscious at three years of age. A typical adult generating delta waves would not be the least bit lucid, however that is not so of children.

Some people think you can't hypnotize a child and there is some truth to that, because children are already hypnotized. With children we can still use hypnosis—we just don't have to go through the same formalities as we would with adults. "Close your eyes imagine Sponge Bob Square Pants. Sponge Bob always brushes his teeth before bed. Sponge Bob wants you to brush your teeth with him, just before bedtime. Is that okay with you?" End of session. This is a bit of a simplified example, but it demonstrates how easy it can be to work with children. The intake portion (history gathering) is much simpler as well, since they don't have much history.

Daydreaming:

Daydreaming is a form of hypnosis and it can lead to more profound states of trance. Daydreaming can help transport (dissociate) us out of every day or uncomfortable life situations. Who hasn't been sitting through some boring lecture daydreaming about being in Acapulco—or another exotic hide-away with our favorite movie star—while sipping on a Mai Tai? That boredom we are escaping from is another form of hypnosis. As hypnotists we make use of boredom as a method of induction. Dr. Milton Erickson used to say that there was no one he couldn't bore into hypnosis.

Driving:

Hypnosis and driving are so closely intertwined it becomes difficult to separate the two. Who hasn't been driving in the car and arrived at their destination and wondered how they got there? Perhaps they don't even recall what route they may have taken. This is hypnosis. The subconscious mind was already programmed with how to drive and how to get there and there was no need for the conscious mind to be involved.

Perhaps you have been driving and missed your exit, or you were heading to a friend's house but instead found yourself pulling into the parking lot at work. This is hypnosis as well. The subconscious has been programmed to do something (like take a certain route to work) and when we begin heading in that general direction, the subconscious takes over and we don't even think about the fact that we need to be going some other direction.

It may be easy to imagine how a person could be driving down the open road, fence posts flitting by the corner of the eye, the hum of the engine lulling him/her into a state of hypnosis. Years ago I read somewhere that eighty-some percent of the time we are driving a car we aren't even aware that we are driving a car. The way some people drive you might wonder if they are even on this planet.

Driving is a very subconscious (hypnotic) experience. We are in our subconscious mind most of the time we are driving. However there was a time when we were driving in the conscious mind; that was when we were learning to drive. Perhaps you had been taking a driver education class, or maybe some well meaning family member or friend was teaching you to drive. Perhaps you recall all of the jerky take offs, the grinding of the gears, and how people were nearly launched through the windshield with every application of the brake peddle. As a traffic light ahead turned to yellow you may have thought to yourself, "Oh, I need to let off of the gas and push in on the clutch as I apply the brake," and the vehicle skidded to a screeching, smoky stop. When the light changed to green, too much gas was then applied as the clutch was released and everyone in the car ended up with whiplash. At 13mph you thought, "It must be time to shift into second gear," while simultaneously grinding the gears and snapping everyone's neck once again. This is driving using the conscious mind.

As time goes on the driving ritual rapidly becomes ingrained in the subconscious mind. When the traffic light begins to change we don't even give a thought as to what needs to happen next. The subconscious is taking care of everything and we automatically begin to let off of the gas and slow down in a smooth, controlled manner. As the light turns green we begin to pull away, automatically and smoothly shifting gears as we proceed to our destination.

There are times when people do try to drive consciously however. I used to work out of a chiropractor's office and much of his practice was built around treating people who were car accident victims. He worked extensively with their insurance companies. Many of these people had problems getting over the trauma of their car accidents, suffered from Post

Traumatic Stress Disorder (PTSD), and found it difficult to drive. It was common for these people to become hyper-vigilant behind the wheel. You have probably noticed some of these people out on the freeway. You might have seen them driving in the left lane at 35 mph—noses pressed against the windshield—obstructing traffic.

These people feel that by remaining vigilantly aware of the traffic around them they will be able to maintain control. The truth is that strategy has the opposite effect. Now they have become a danger to themselves and to everyone around them. As a hypnotist my job is getting these people to relax and back to the place where they are once again driving in the subconscious mind and actually enjoying the process.

The idea of driving in the car and not being consciously aware may seem a bit scary to some people, however we do a much better job when we are in that subconscious (trance) state. We actually have a greater sensory awareness of the entire (peripheral) world around us in the subconscious mind. Who hasn't been driving down the road daydreaming about Fabio or Fabrina, when for no apparent reason you look over and see something happening and are able to avoid an accident? This type of sensory experience does not occur with someone driving 35 mph, nose jammed into the windshield, experiencing the world through tunnel-vision.

It's the subconscious mind that allows us to drive down the freeway steering with our knees while simultaneously talking on the cell phone, eating a Whopper and smoking a cigarette. Never mind the low oil warning buzzer that is going off, just turn the volume up on the radio some more.

Shock:

Shock is a form of hypnosis. When a tragic accident has occurred people will stand around with a blank look on their faces and do nothing in the middle of a situation that requires action. It is not that these people are stupid or uncaring. It is simply that they have no paradigms to operate within for such situations. A total bypass of their critical faculty has just occurred and they have no operating models to use as a reference point. These people are totally hypnotized and if someone has their wits about them and starts giving directions, these people will gladly follow. Their minds want something to make sense, but they don't know what to do in this situation. If someone starts yelling out instructions such as, "You call 911, you get some blankets, and you, help move this debris!" and so on, they will respond.

We can use shock more formally in hypnosis by saying or doing things that don't fit conventional paradigms about how the world is supposed to work. Misdirection is a way to achieve this without the necessity of a tragic accident. A bypass of the critical faculty is still achieved and the subconscious will take suggestions directly just so the world will make sense once again.

Meditation:

How does meditation differ from hypnosis? I have been a student of various methods of meditation in the past. So what separates hypnosis from meditation? Hypnosis and meditation are not two different things at all. Meditation is an application of hypnosis—a way to access and apply hypnosis—nothing more, nothing less. This does not detract from its profound benefits.

Skilled meditators can achieve all levels of consciousness and accomplish amazing feats. But to say that meditation is something totally different and unique compared to hypnosis is not correct. Meditation is a method for accessing hypnosis. Meditation (another form of trance) in some form or another has been around for a very long time and represents a practical application of trance. Hypnosis is a much broader term which envelopes meditation as part of what hypnosis is.

Some individuals may have a great attachment to one term or another and would like to defend their position as being superior. I feel that one term is not superior but complementary to the other.

Conditioned Response:

Conditioned response, which was the focus of Salter's book *What is Hypnosis,* is (you guessed it) another form of hypnosis. This subject is dealt with more in depth in its own chapter further in this book. Also see my earlier book *The Power of the Past* for information about anchors and triggers since they are virtually the same.

Staring into Space:

Have you ever caught yourself just staring off into space and noticing how good it feels? Perhaps you hoped that no one would notice or distract you so that you could just remain in this comforting state. My example earlier in this chapter of gazing up at the clouds floating in the sky is an example of staring off into space. This is another of the many faces of hypnosis.

A variation of that is staring into a fire, like a campfire or fireplace, or staring at the flickering flame of a candle.

Repetition:

Repetition is a form of hypnosis. When we perform the same task over and over (much like in the earlier example of driving) it becomes ingrained in our subconscious mind until we can continue that task without even giving it a thought. Certainly when people perform repetitious tasks on the job it's easy for the mind to wander off somewhere else while at the same time the job is being done. People even say, "I could do my job in my sleep," and they literally almost could. Certainly a secretary who is used to typing away for hours every day is off in a trance and may not even have a clue what has just been typed.

My mother (who was not into housework at all) was quite content doing the ironing. She would become calm and peaceful and go off into a meditation (hypnosis) while doing the ironing.

When we are doing a repetitive exercise such as the elliptical machine, or rowing machine, or the stationary bike, we can go off into a trance. Maybe you have been exercising this way at times and been amazed to look down and see just how long you had been engaged in your workout. This type of exercising is particularly beneficial as a form of stress relief.

Repetition occurs in many other areas as well. Advertisers know that through repetition their product becomes ingrained in your subconscious mind. Have you ever noticed that at election time there are little signs stuck in people's lawns and nailed to phone poles that read *Yes on 13*. Who even knows what 13 is? But everywhere you turn you see *Yes on 13*. When we show up at the polls and see amendment 13 on the ballet do we stop and think, gee, *Yes on 13*, that really speaks to my heart and who I am as a thinking, caring human being? Or do we just push that button where it says *Yes on 13* because we have been programmed to do so through repetition? Could it be that the group behind *Yes on 13* just has more money and more of those little signs than the group who is behind *No on 13*?

How many times have you heard some sixty second commercial that repeats the product's name or phone number sixty times until it just drives you nuts? Even the irritation the advertiser has created in you is a form of hypnosis. We may not like it, but the repetition gets our attention focused on their product.

Expectancy:

Expectancy is a form of hypnosis. What we expect to happen is what tends to happen (a kind of waking hypnosis) and I talk about expectancy more in the section on waking hypnosis. Expectancy is a huge force in hypnosis.

Storytelling:

Much the same way a TV show can engage your attention, a good story teller can create a powerful hypnosis. If I am telling a story that is very scary or has to do with surviving in extreme cold temperatures in a harsh environment I can get goose bumps to rise on your skin (a subconscious, hypnotic, response). I mention more about this phenomenon in the chapter on waking hypnosis.

Imagination:

Imagination plays a huge role in hypnosis. Daydreaming, storytelling, guided visualization, self hypnosis processes, and more all make use of imagination (which is a purely subconscious activity).

The following is taken from my book *No Time to Waist—Powerful Hypnosis Weight Loss Secrets You Need to Know*:

Often people don't take the imagination seriously. However, anything of any importance begins with the imagination. Perhaps you are sitting in some sort of building right now reading this book. Perhaps that building is your home, office, classroom, or a bookstore, or some similar type of building. You are sitting in that building right this very moment because of imagination. There was a day when someone thought that a building might be necessary to serve certain purposes. That person imagined in their mind what that building might be like and what might need to be included in it. One day that person probably went to an architect and told that architect what he or she had imagined in his/her mind. The architect then imagined in his mind what that might be like. Together they began creating onto paper what they had imagined. One day the architect gave that paper to a contractor. The contractor imagined in his mind how he was going to lay everything out, and how he would bring in all of the materials and subcontractors and utilities, until, one day, you are sitting in that building reading this book. And believe me, there was a day when I imagined you sitting there reading this book. So I have a very powerful imagination, for I have created you.

What we can imagine we can create. If you've ever watched the Olympics you might recall the award ceremonies. Athletes are awarded gold, silver or bronze medals. Long before that winning athlete received the gold medal, thousands of times he or she imagined standing up there on the platform and receiving that medal. I'm sure the bronze medalist had imagined that as well. But the point is that athlete would have never gotten there by imagining finishing in forty-seventh place. Believe me, if you want to reach your goal, whether it's reaching your desired weight or publishing a book about weight, it requires positive imagination around achieving your goal.

"Logic will get you from A to B; imagination will take you everywhere."

—*Albert Einstein*

Placebo:

The placebo effect is waking suggestion and waking hypnosis at its finest. Refer to the sections in this book that address waking hypnosis, waking suggestion, and expectancy for more detailed information. Although hypnosis has many faces the placebo effect and hypnosis are one and the same. Placebo is a method of applying hypnosis. This is a broad subject and has its own chapter in this book.

Massage:

Have you ever been having a massage and found yourself off somewhere else the whole time? Even though Guido was shoving his elbow through the ribs in your back, and manipulating your sternum from the back side, you were oblivious. This is hypnosis as well.

One massage therapist who we see even goes to the extent of giving positive suggestions while he is working away.

Getting your hair and nails done or going to a tanning salon is relevant here as well. So often when we are pampering ourselves or being pampered it is easy to zone out and go off into our own little trance world. Whatever the value of tanning salons might be, I think the one benefit that doesn't seem to be promoted is the fact that getting into the tanning bed causes us to close our eyes and shut up and do nothing for thirty minutes. I encourage pampering moments to de-stress and allow the mind wander.

Taking a walk:

Taking a walk can have effects similar to a massage and/or those pampering moments. My wife and I walk the dogs every day and often it's very late at night. There is a wilderness area right across from where we live and the late night walks through there are very peaceful and relaxing, and allow for reflecting, away from the hustle and bustle and business of our daily lives. While taking walks many thoughts and ideas for these pages have come to my mind.

Boredom:

Boredom is a form of hypnosis. Have you ever become so bored during a class or a meeting or listening to someone or a TV program that you became distracted? Boredom is also a method that we use to hypnotize people.

Eating:

Oh my God! I'm eating due to hypnosis? Well certainly eating and hypnosis are connected. Eating can be a purely subconscious habit response. Have you ever eaten just because it was noon, or because "we always eat at 6:00 around here" or did you stop and think "well it is noon but I'm not really hungry, I'll just wait a couple of hours (not likely)? Do you ever come home at the end of day and go straight to the refrigerator? Did you say to yourself, "Gee, I'm really hungry and I need something to eat," or did you just go and open the fridge because that is what you did yesterday and the day before that? Don't people find themselves eating the same kinds of foods over and over because that is what they have always done? Guess what? That is hypnosis as well.

Let's go a little further with the eating and hypnosis thing. Have you ever heard people referring to certain foods as comfort foods? Have you ever stopped to wonder why that is? We create a subconscious (hypnotic) connection with certain foods. If every Sunday the whole family got together and mom fixed her usual pot roast or baked ham or fried chicken the feelings associated with that experience (anchor) continue to be associated even when mom and the family are no longer around. Now whenever we have pot roast or ham or fried chicken those same good feelings come back (trigger).

We have other hypnotic connections with eating as well. When you go to the ball game are you thinking about how hungry you are and that you need to get proper nutrients into your body soon or do you just order a chili dog and beer because that's what you always do? Is going to the movies a highly physical activity that causes us to get hungry or is the smell of popcorn triggering some old hypnotic response in us? When you walk into someone's home and cake is being served do you scrutinize what your level of hunger is in that moment to determine if you need to take in nutrients? Or do you just indulge in the cake because it's there or you think it is the polite thing to do?

After winning the little league game we all go to the Dairy Queen to celebrate so feeling good and Dairy Queen are now associated. There is also the fact that those foods that are high in fat, sugar or carbohydrates trigger certain feel good chemical responses within us and if we are feeling out of sorts we subconsciously gravitate to those kinds of foods that will cause us to have "feel good" sensations.

Herd Mentality:

We are herd (pack) animals and with that comes a kind of hypnosis. We get warm, fuzzy feelings when we are doing the same things as the rest of the herd; eating the same kinds of foods, living in similar kinds of shelters, raising families, cheering for our side. We do these things because it has worked in the past (part of our nature) and because subconsciously it's easier to go with the flow.

In the past this sort of strategy gave people a certain amount of safety and security, and therefore we lived to pass those genes on and the cycle continues. However it doesn't always make sense to follow the herd hypnosis, especially if what the herd is doing is detrimental. Going to fast food restaurants or eating highly processed foods or voting for the same political party as your friends or being a Cubs fan are just a few examples. Unfortunately for many people it is easier to follow along with the group than to break away and try something different.

This is actually an area where hypnosis can be very helpful because it lets us shift some of those patterns and makes it possible to do things that are different from the rest of the herd. This is often what it takes to make positive changes, especially with things like our eating habits. If we do the same things the rest of the herd is doing we will get the same results that the rest of the herd is getting.

The Reptilian Brain:

The reptilian part of the brain is a very basic primal part of the brain and it loves to do the same thing over and over (sound anything like the subconscious?). All higher animals from lizards on up have this part of the brain.

This is, generally speaking, how it works. One day the lizard crawled from his hole and slithered down the hill until he ran into a pond. While he was at the pond he caught some bugs and got some water. Then the lizard went back up the hill the way he came, and back to his hole. Now every day the lizard crawls down the hill to the pond and catches some bugs and heads back to his hole just like before. This cycle gets repeated over and over again. Why? Because it works. If you go into the mountains or countryside you will find trails through the brush or the forest. Why? Because the trail led to a beneficial destination and it worked. Once animals went that way, maybe deer or cattle or some other animals, it worked. Now they go the same way and over and over again until a trail forms. Because it worked. It doesn't even need to be pretty; we just need to survive because to the reptilian brain if it worked once it will work again, and the fact that we survived is proof <u>enough</u> that it works.

We do the same things over and over as well. We like to go to the same restaurants and sit at the same table or park in the same parking spaces, or take the same route to work. We send our kids to the same college we went to. Why? Because it worked. The reptilian brain is a way that we create habit which is a nice segue into my next subject.

Habit:

Habits are formed in the subconscious through repetition. Once something becomes a habit we will continue to do it over and over again because it is easy.

Habits can be our friend or our worst enemy. If we develop good habits, like going to the gym four times a week, they will work in our favor. If we develop bad habits, like eating fast food all the time, then they will work against us.

Because habits are part of the subconscious we pay no penalty in the form of stress; however trying to consciously change a habit does create stress and that's one reason why it becomes difficult for people to do so.

We have a saying in the hypnosis field: "When the conscious and the subconscious are in conflict, the subconscious will always win." That's because the subconscious pays no stress for its part. The subconscious just continues doing the same old thing over and over. It takes conscious effort (stress) for us to overcome the habit and the conscious will most likely lose.

Have you ever walked into a room and flipped the light switch and the lights were already on? Because the subconscious has reached for that light switch so many times before it just automatically does it again. No thought or stress is involved in reaching for the light switch, it just happens automatically (reflex response).

It's best to teach our children good habits right from the start and that will make everyone's life a lot easier. Through hypnosis and the access we gain to the subconscious mind we can end up at the health food store instead of the drive through window.

Psychosomatic Phenomenon:

"It's all in your head." We've probably all heard that statement before, whether it was being applied to us or to someone else. It could have been a comment from a doctor or some well meaning friend or relative. The statement implies that because some symptom that is being experienced has no physical basis, then it's just in the head so "get over it," As if what is going on in the head is not valid. The truth is that a lot more is going on in terms of physical symptoms due to our head (emotions) than most people would care to admit.

We know and accept that certain physical issues like blood pressure, ulcers, heart rate, etc. are often the result of an emotional, stress-related issue, yet usually we don't say, "Oh, well, it's just in your head." We tend to take these things more seriously, perhaps because they are treatable through medications and surgery, yet that doesn't necessarily mean they are not in the head (subconscious).

Psychosomatic phenomenon is the relationship (interdependence) between mental and physical phenomena. It is not necessarily a bad thing but that is what pops into our minds when we hear the term. Our psychosomatic experience could be that we have a very strong, healthy genetic heritage and that we will live a long healthy life. On the other hand we may believe that because our father had a heart attack and died early, and his father did as well, that we need to be getting our estate in order in preparation for our demise. The fact that our predecessors lived on a diet of ribs and pork rinds, were two hundred pounds overweight, and smoked, doesn't seem to mean much to us.

My brother and father both had coronary issues and both had angioplasties. Both had very high cholesterol and were overweight and had been heavy smokers. They both resigned themselves to the fact that heart disease was fairly eminent in their futures and did little to prevent it. There were no problems genetically. My father's parents had lived to a ripe old age with very few health issues. Even my father—who did not take good care of himself—died at the age of 83 of <u>un</u>natural causes.

I, on the other hand, have been just the opposite. Due to my much healthier, active, vegetarian lifestyle I enjoy having a cholesterol count way below the national average and have never had any serious health issue or weight problems. It all has to do with our psychosomatic profiles.

What about things like headaches and other pains? What if we wake up every morning with a headache or every time there is a business meeting or family function there is that headache? The doctors have checked us out and done MRI's and there are no physical causes for the discomfort yet we continue to suffer and again we get the *it's all in your head* answer. Yes, it is in my head and I can feel it (and it is very real). Just because it's "in your head" does not mean that it is not real or that it is less important. It is hypnotic in origin however. While we call ourselves hypnotists or hypnotherapists the truth is a lot of what we are really doing is dehypnotizing people from the hypnosis that they have already unknowingly received. That is one reason I believe hypnosis is so effective with so many different things: We are fighting fire with fire, so to speak. Since hypnosis brought on the (psychosomatic) issues then hypnosis should be the logical cure as well.

If our issue is headaches and there is no organic cause then maybe they have occurred through hypnosis. At some point we got used to the fact (created an association) that certain situations resulted in a headache and because it happened before then it certainly will happen again. And so it does happen again even if it does not need to. In the early 70's I suffered from migraines. I would do well through the work week while I was under some stress, but as soon as the weekend came along I would have a migraine again until Monday. It is likely that having those migraines served me in some way (secondary gain) or maybe the universe had a bigger plan for me and this was my gateway. I say that because those migraines played a large part in leading me toward hypnosis. I learned hypnotic methods to get rid of the migraines and I have been migraine free ever since.

Other pain could be working for us in similar ways; who as a child didn't learn that faking a stomach ache would get us out of that exam tomorrow? And who hasn't observed that when you really need that stomach ache to work in your favor it will occur?

I have worked extensively with pain issues. I like working with phantom pain the best. This is pain that has no possible physical reason to exist. For instance, someone has had their foot removed yet still feels the pain in that foot. One young woman I worked with was suffering with back pain. She had been injured as child and the surgeons had repaired the damage, however she continued to experience the same pain. The surgeons went back in and froze the nerves that are associated with sending the signal of pain to the brain from that area of the body. The process of freezing the nerve causes it to die. Yet she continued to feel the pain. It would be similar to me talking to you on the telephone and someone cutting the phone lines, yet we continued to talk. What I believe often happens in these cases is that the mind becomes so accustomed (expectancy/hypnotized) to dealing with pain that it continues to do so even though there is no logical reason for it.

When that young woman came into my office I asked her if she could touch her toes. She tried, but she could not even get close to her toes. After her session not only could she easily reach down and touch her toes, she was free of all discomfort.

Many things I deal with daily are the results of hypnosis (conditioning) we received that we weren't aware of, and certainly didn't think of as hypnosis. Phobias, PTSD, and all sorts of emotional issues are the result of hypnosis. Sometimes that hypnosis was the complete bypass of the critical faculty such as might have occurred with PTSD, or for a phobia sufferer. Other times it may be a result of some underlying messages that we received.

Yes it may be "just in your head" but that doesn't mean that it's not real and that doesn't mean that something can't be easily done about it.

Prayer:

Yes, praying is hypnosis, but only when it is done mindfully. When little Johnny is bouncing around the bedroom repeating *Now I lay me down to sleep* with his eyes closed, his hands together, but still in motion he is not praying. When prayer is done with mindful intention and time, it becomes hypnosis.

My good friend and colleague Father James Martino says that prayer is meant to take half an hour. He also says that prayer is us talking to God and meditation is us listening to God. I believe those two things (prayer and meditation) to be more closely related than some would care to admit. However you might want to view them both can be a positive influence in our lives.

Prayer beads (and there are various methods that apply similar use of beads) are a part of the meditative (hypnotic) process in some instances. The beads become a focus, a sort of physical mantra that helps the user to stay connected with his/her intention.

Altered States of Consciousness:

Any altered state of consciousness is hypnosis. Altered states of consciousness include any state of awareness that deviates from our normal state of consciousness, and that range is huge. Altered states can mean anything from taking a cat nap to having an emergency room physician activating a defibrillator while we are in the midst of a severe drug overdose.

Whether you are the guest of honor at a surprise birthday party or are watching your home burn to the ground you are in an altered state of consciousness (hypnosis). Shooting the white water rapids, jumping out of an airplane, riding the roller coasters at Six Flags, down on one knee proposing marriage, or running from the authorities we are in an altered state.

While some people work hard to enter altered states through meditation, music, Whirling Dervish dancing or some spiritually awakening drug, others are trying to escape the altered state that to them represents an emotional prison. Isn't depression an altered state and wouldn't a lot of people like to change that state? Aren't the medications we use to escape these altered states (to achieve "normalcy") just creating another altered state? Isn't there a point when depression is no longer and altered state but our normal state of being?

What is normal? This question opens a new can of worms. For normal to exist there would have to be a consensus on a definition and the subjective nature (our perceptions) offers scant hope of that. Perhaps normal isn't all it's cracked up to be anyway.

Shamanism:

Shamans could well be the first users of formal hypnosis. Shamanism is a broad term for ancient through modern healers. Medicine men and women are shamans that we have a model for, but this term applies to a variety of healers.

Shamans make use of a wide variety of ceremonies and rituals, music (drumming), chanting, herbs, potions, and incantations to achieve healing results, all of which are anchored in hypnosis. More will be found on this topic further on in this chapter and in the chapter on Waking Hypnosis.

Sleep:

While as hypnotists we work hard to create a distinction between hypnosis and sleep, isn't sleep another state of hypnosis (certainly it's an altered state of consciousness)? When working in hypnosis we try to avoid associating sleep and hypnosis, and ideally we work in hypnosis and not sleep (for the most part).

It does seem curious to me that we can be at the same levels of consciousness (brain wave activity) and be in hypnosis or we can be asleep. I have experimented with myself over and over on this one while dropping off to sleep at night. There seems to be very different feelings associated with sleeping and with being in a formal hypnotic trance. I wish I could describe the exact sensations that distinguish those two experiences but the problem is that when I'm asleep enough to experience the sensations the conscious mind is nowhere around to make note of it. Which is probably why it is sleep and not something else.

Sleep, for lack of any better definition, is the suspension of conscious activity. I know that there are times when I am working with someone in hypnosis and I would love to create a suspension of any conscious activity (for the client) for it can sometimes be an obstruction. We do use sleep for hypnotic purposes however and people can be suggestible while they sleep. Sleep is certainly an altered state so it seems logical that sleep is hypnosis even if it doesn't lend itself as well to therapeutic practices.

Find more on sleep in the chapter *Conditioned Response.*

Ceremony and Ritual:

From drumming to chanting, dancing and sacrifices, ceremony and ritual play a huge role in hypnosis. Medicine men, witch doctors, and shamans of all types have relied on ceremony and ritual necessary to create hypnosis that will lead to the healing effects desired. Faith healers are hypnotists more than anything else. By going through the ceremony leading up to the healing everyone becomes hypnotized and open to the possibilities. Once the faith healer does his magic on the first sufferer and that person is left squirming and squealing on the stage after regaining the ability to walk, the following participants become putty in the healer's hands. Seeing the first person being healed creates the expectation that this will happen again; and so it does (much like the fire walk I will discuss in the waking hypnosis chapter).

Ceremony and ritual play a role in many other ways as well, each time creating an associated hypnosis. My brother went to John Elway Honda to have his marriage certificate notarized and while that "ceremony" didn't elicit the emotion of a more traditional wedding, he was just as married in the eyes of the law. Certainly the hypnosis around my brother's marriage was much different than that created for Princess Diana and Prince Charles.

Graduating from high school, college or law school are all associated with ceremony and hypnosis. And so does potty training and going to kindergarten; or the ceremony of the judge entering the courtroom. Many cultures have rituals (sadly missing in our culture) that bring young men into adulthood. I say men not so as to exclude women but because women have natural changes that signal movement into adulthood more so than men do.

Political activities are rife with ritual from the signing of the Declaration of Independence to political conventions, inaugurations and state of the nation speeches. Ribbon cutting ceremonies, shoveling the first scoop of dirt to symbolize the start of a new project, driving the first spike of a new railroad, or signing a significant law into effect are ritualistic also.

Purchasing a new home has all sorts of rituals to go through right up to signing the final papers and receiving the keys.

Ceremony and ritual are the waking hypnosis that help to create the expectation that something different is occurring or is about to occur. We use ceremony and ritual in our hypnosis sessions. For example, leading someone into a past life requires a ceremony to make it believable or acceptable to the mind. If I were to say, "Okay, you are there, tell me what is happening," I might not get much of a response, but because we have gone through an imaginative, scene-setting ceremony, the expectation has occurred that something different is now happening.

Emotions:

It is easy to realize that when we are in an emotional state we are in a trance state—a trance state that can vary widely.

Have you ever fallen in love or observed someone who has fallen in love? We will say and do things and agree to do things in this state that would seem to fly in the face of common sense, yet we are accepting of this unusual behavior (perhaps due to the *trance logic,* see glossary). Falling in love may be an extreme example of happiness (joy), but any experience of an enjoyable kind is yet another of the variations of hypnosis.

Excitement can also vary widely from the anticipation of an upcoming birthday party to hanging by our fingernails from a cliff. Excitement, fear and terror are close cousins. Have you ever gotten on a major amusement park ride like a roller coaster? There is excitement just being at the amusement park with all of the crowds and sounds and sensory stimulation going on. We take that excitement to a new level when we decide to get in line for the giant coaster ride. Getting locked into our seat brings the excitement up a notch as we anticipate the start of the ride. As the ride begins to move we rise to an even greater level of excitement and realize there is no turning back now. Zooming down the rails it becomes a blur of emotions, excitement, fear, terror and exhilaration. In those moments when an unexpected turn or loop occurs we may well have the bypass of the critical faculty and an opportunity to give suggestions to the subconscious mind. However it is likely that the hypnotherapist sitting next to you is too terrified to come up with a good suggestion. There is no doubt in my mind that hypnosis is occurring all over the place in a moment like this.

What about other emotions that are not so fun? Sadness, depression, anger, hatred, and grief are all strong emotions that evoke their own unique trance state. In my book *The Power of the Past* I talk about how strong emotions can pull someone into a somnambulistic state. The emotions help the therapist to keep the subject in the subconscious mind so that the therapy continues smoothly. These emotions can be an aid to the therapist however. Even when the individual is not in the therapist's office hypnosis is still being triggered whenever they have these feelings on their own.

It only stands to reason that all therapeutic modalities employ hypnosis (whether or not the therapist is aware of it) simply due to the clients' own emotions. This could work to the advantage of the therapeutic session. Wouldn't it be nice if all therapists had a better understanding of hypnosis and how to take advantage of these moments?

Guided Visualization:

Guided visualization is a process that is used widely even by people who do not call themselves hypnotists. Therapists and trainers of all sorts have lead groups on visual journeys to help achieve some goal. It could be for some abundance process, metaphysical type journey, health issues or stress issues, etc. Usually the process begins with a simple induction such as a progressive relaxation or sometimes there is no induction at all.

Often the leader doesn't realize that he/she is using hypnosis and may even call it something else. If asked he/she may say that it is not hypnosis, but just an imagination exercise. No matter what the leader of the visualization may call it, and no matter what their particular title might be, it is still hypnosis.

Religion:

While we may not think of religion as being hypnosis, hypnosis plays a big role. From the waking hypnosis that is created simply by being in a place of worship or around the clergy whom we idolize, to actual ceremonies and rituals that create hypnotic experiences (worship is a hypnotic experience). The fact that we are associating ourselves with others who have like minded beliefs helps to create feelings—an ambiance (waking hypnosis).

Some people may take offense at such comparisons, but it is our fear of the unknown that creates prejudice. It is my hope that these ideas will help encourage the acceptance of all belief systems and thus enable us to more fully embrace one another's diversity.

The Metaphysical:

I would like to lump the metaphysical in with religion and I know this might upset some metaphysicians because many of them are attempting to distance themselves from traditional religious beliefs. The truth is that anything that we believe in strongly, and that serves us and helps to define our aspirations, is a religion whether it centers on Christ or Buddha, Jim Jones, a higher power or the almighty dollar. Even being an atheist becomes a religion when we hold it as a strong belief that supports us and who we believe we are on this planet. Even though we may not accept a God per se, our beliefs can become God-like.

Hypnosis by its very nature tends to be metaphysical, but some will take it to the sublime. There may well be a place for that however it becomes an area where people's belief systems can be offended. It is better and safer to stick with more conventional therapeutic methods when working with the general public.

Various Therapies:

In the chapter on waking hypnosis and the placebo effect I will discuss how hypnosis plays a big role in the practice of modern medicine. The unrealized use and practice of hypnosis is occurring in all sorts of therapies.

Psychotherapists are using hypnosis all the time in their practices whether or not they are aware of it. Just sitting and talking with someone, especially when that person is emotional, is an altered state of consciousness. As I talk about in my book *The Power of the Past*, emotions pull us into trance (hypnosis). This is when therapies are at their best. I believe that much of the benefit people receive from therapy occurs due to the hypnosis that takes place unintentionally during the work. All psychotherapists would do well to have a good understanding of hypnosis and to learn how to make better use of it.

Sigmund Freud is considered the father of modern psychotherapy but what people don't usually realize is that he began his psychotherapy career as a hypnotist. Freud learned from some of the better hypnotists of his time, most notably Charcot. Freud was not the first to venture into the world of modern psychotherapy. Janet was probably the most prolific user of hypnosis for psychotherapy at that time and then Charcot, Braid and Bernhiem among others.

When Freud abandoned hypnosis (his hypnosis skills were not particularly good, especially in the area of rapport) he began using free association methods. The old images of Freud sitting with his back to his client while they lay on the coach talking with him are accurate. Contemporary hypnotists would consider sitting with your back toward someone very poor rapport. Yet it is not very difficult to imagine Freud sitting there talking with someone on the couch, and to suppose that they might drift off into a hypnotic trance during the process. Of course it is likely that they would be talking about some emotional issues and that would also help to pull them into a trance state. Through all of this it is possible that some people actually received some benefit with their therapy.

When I was studying Gestalt Therapy at the Gestalt Institute of the Rockies I became aware that gestalt clients were in hypnosis and benefiting from it, even if the facilitator of the session didn't have a clue.

Other therapies have hypnosis working for them as well. When an acupuncturist pokes a needle in us designed to affect some beneficial change it could well be that the healing occurs due to the waking hypnosis or placebo effect.

When we are treated by a chiropractor or are given some remedy from an herbalist, could it be that, once again, the hypnosis is causing the positive change?

Even seeing a psychic has a similar effect. If the psychic tells us we are going to meet someone new in the next few months and we do, does that mean that they were really seeing into the future or did they just set our mind up (expectation) to allow someone to show up for us?

Whether or not you choose to believe in psychics they can provide useful, inexpensive psychotherapy. Sometimes just having someone to talk to can be very therapeutic. If we perceive that person to have some special powers (waking hypnosis) and they tell us things are going to be fine in the next two weeks (expectation) and that helps us to get through, is there anything wrong with that? Is a licensed psychiatrist doing any better?

We could lump witches, tarot card readers, palm readers, astrologers, etc. into this category as well. This is not to say that their particular modality does or does not have merit on its own, only that hypnosis is playing a major role.

Some people might assume that I take issue with other kinds of therapies but that is not the case. I believe in and use all of the modalities that I have talked about, and I refer clients out to other types of therapists regularly. I do probably view such practices from a somewhat different perspective, however.

Music:

Yes, music is hypnosis whether you are getting lost in the hard driving beat of some rock band or caught up in the emotion of a ballad. Have you ever been driving along listening to your favorite radio station when a song comes on that takes you right back to 1958 and the high school prom with Betty Sue? That's a form of hypnosis that we call anchors and triggers. Once we create an association with one thing then that thing will continue to trigger that association. It is not unlike reflex response or conditioned (Pavlovian) response.

What if you happen to be the musician? Then a whole different hypnosis is occurring because skilled musicians are entering a trance state while playing, and in response their audience experiences its own hypnosis as well.

Like driving the car, playing an instrument when you started out took a lot of very conscious effort that included screeching strings and missed notes that had dogs all over town howling for mercy. However, after devoted practice the activity became a subconscious experience to the point that skilled musicians can pick up an instrument and play it at will.

Witchcraft:

While the term witchcraft conjures up all sorts of images of evil, ugly women riding through the moonlight on broomsticks, casting evil spells and giving children poisoned apples, those images are for the most part inaccurate.

Witchcraft got a bad rap during the time of the Inquisition when people (mostly women) were being hanged, burned at the stake, drowned and guillotined for any sort of suspicious behavior.

The truth is that the people we refer to as witches were those who were involved in using folk remedies to help their families and communities. Many of these remedies included potions and tonics. A big part of what they did was through rituals including sacred circles, burning candles, dances, incantations (waking hypnosis) and the use of symbols. While there can be a dark side to any practice and belief, witchcraft is by far a positive influence even today. I would venture to say that witchcraft is more alive today in Salem, Massachusetts than it was at the time of the witch trials. Some witches practice today as midwives, doulas, and healers.

Brain Washing:

Any effort aimed at instilling specific attitudes and beliefs in a person can be called brain washing. While the term brain washing conjures up all sorts of images of bamboo being shoved under the fingernails or water drip torture, and on and on, that ain't necessarily so. Yes, that can be a part of brain washing, however, sometimes captured enemies were treated very favorably and were won over by their captors who befriended them and created trust. As time went on, their captors caused them to doubt their own troops (government, friends, etc.) which worked to win their allegiance.

By this definition advertising, political campaigns, educational systems, propaganda and religions could all be said to employ brain washing. It does not imply that this is good or bad, but just that it exists. In some ways this should go under the chapter on *The Fear of Hypnosis* because for the most part this is the hypnosis to be concerned about; that is to say the hypnosis that occurs without our awareness. Which segues us neatly into the next topic.

Advertising:

Advertising makes big use of hypnosis and in a wide variety of ways. One way is through simple suggestions that we hear over and over and that cause a compounding effect. Often advertisers are using very good hypnotic language; in fact we often refer to advertising and sales literature to formulate suggestions. Many of these suggestions are given through clever (or obnoxious) little jingles that continue to rattle around in our heads even though we wish they wouldn't.

Creating associations between their product and something that we find desirable is a common advertising strategy. For instance, associations with being young, healthy or sexy are often linked to smoking, sodas and alcoholic beverages, or whatever the latest miracle pill might be.

Years ago I worked for a large county, repairing their trucks and construction machinery. One of the vendor catalogs we had on hand featured an attractive model in a bikini lying on top of a Dempsey Dumpster trash compactor. I wondered what in the world that young woman had to do with trash trucks, but to the advertiser it didn't matter; he knew that the people who buy trash trucks also like girls in bikinis, and while that association might seem like a stretch, it still works.

My wife and I were driving downtown with some other hypnotist friends who were from out of town. We were passing a billboard with a very seductive looking woman on it when my friend commented, "Why would they feel the need to do that?" My response was, "It got you to look." Sex in advertising is everywhere and there is one good reason for it: it works. Primates are the most sexual beings on earth and subconsciously we respond to anything sexual.

Lynsi and I were in a Florida restaurant having lunch with Steven Parkhill, author of *Answer Cancer* a well known treatise on his use of hypnosis for cancer. Steven had begun his career in sales and he showed us examples right on the menu of how pictures of cocktails had been subliminally imbued with sexual shapes just so our minds would create that connection.

Lately I have noticed some trends in advertising and the use of hypnosis. I notice more advertisements where several things (conversation) are happening at the same time. While the main focus is on the activity that is occurring in the foreground, there is another seemingly dissimilar activity occurring in the background. If you listen to what is being said the different conversation in the background is constantly timed in such a way as to support important statements that are occurring in the primary part of the ad. This creates a sort of embedded suggestion, just the sort of technique we use in hypnosis, to support and make the statements that are occurring in the foreground more powerful.

Another thing I have noticed is that something totally outrageous happens in connection with a product. In a recent chewing gum ad, someone comes up to the person chewing this gum and sucks it right out of their mouth, and then the product is displayed again. It could be that advertisers are blatantly attempting to get a bypass of the critical faculty to gain direct access to the subconscious with their message.

Just sitting and looking at the TV causes a hypnotic effect (eye fixation) which causes us to be more suggestible. Combine that with compounding of suggestions by advertisers and soon cash registers are ringing all over the country.

I'm sure when it comes to advertising and hypnosis I have just scratched the surface here.

Yawning:

Have you ever noticed that when one person starts to yawn, others in the room will then start to yawn as well. Maybe you try to resist, but you can feel the urge to yawn. The yawn becomes a sort of non-verbal suggestion.

Vomiting:

Perhaps as a youngster you were in the classroom or on the school bus when someone vomited. Even though you were feeling fine just moments before, now you feel those sickening sensations arise. Perhaps another youngster actually does vomit as a result. Because certain feelings were anchored with the sounds and smells of that particular activity they now come to the surface quite easily. Like yawning, there is a non-verbal suggestion occurring as well. Adults have a similar response, but often we have become desensitized to it over the years.

Sex:

Finally! I've got your attention. Yes, sex is just (well maybe not just) another face of hypnosis. It would be no stretch to say that when having sex we are in an altered state. You can become oblivious to the fact that a police officer is shining a light through the car window, or that your date's Rottweiler is gnawing your leg off (an indication of somnambulism). If you are not totally absorbed during sex and find yourself thinking about business or the kids or some other duties, you are doing it wrong. Relax; enjoy it, allow yourself to be mesmerized. So hopefully this hypnosis thing is starting to sound better all the time.

Voodoo:

Voodoo establishes a kind of waking hypnosis. It can work well within certain cultures where there is a strong belief in its power. If someone believes that a voodoo spell has been put on them, the spell could have the negative effects it was intended to have; a sort of nocebo response. It would seem unlikely that someone in some other part of the world that I had no connection to (or belief in their system) could stick a pin in a doll and create some negative response in me. Voodoo requires a sort of co-dependency to be effective.

Pretend:

Pretending is a form of hypnosis. If we pretend strongly enough we create a trance state. A type of hypnotic induction is called the *pretend method* or *act as if.* Simply by asking someone to pretend they are hypnotized actually has the effect of causing them to be hypnotized.

Dr. James Elliotson was discredited by the British Medical establishment when he demonstrated the amputation of a man's leg in front of other physicians. Other doctors claimed that the man must have been trained in some way to not show any pain. Well that would be a nice trick, but regardless the use of hypnosis would have been in effect. If the man was acting (pretending) to not experience the pain it would still be due to hypnotic effect, however at that time not enough was known about hypnosis to explain the phenomenon to the close minded medical community of the day. One thing I would be certain of is that Elliotson had gained the bypass of the critical faculty of those doctors.

The Egg on the Cover of This Book:

The glass egg on the cover of this book is hypnosis—a kind of waking hypnosis—a non-verbal suggestion.

When I was a kid some farmers would make use of these glass eggs (and some still do). When a new batch of hens was reaching maturity, but hadn't started laying eggs yet, the farmer would place these glass eggs in some of the chickens' nests, and lo and behold the chickens would start laying eggs. Yes, the farmers were basically hypnotizing the chickens, giving them a non-verbal suggestion. Once one chicken starts to lay eggs then the rest will get into the process (mass hypnosis). I don't believe the farmer was getting a bypass of the critical faculty with the chickens, and I'm not sure that there would be much to bypass with a chicken, but certainly the waking hypnosis was doing its job.

When we place decoys on a lake it causes water fowl to land on that body of water. Isn't this a form of non-verbal suggestion (albeit a deceitful one) much like the brooding eggs?

So what isn't hypnosis?

From taking a shower to worship services; rising in the morning to a day at work or school, working at the computer, running, reading, tuning out your spouse, using a sweat lodge, a sauna, or being absorbed in anything, it would be hard to come up with something in our life that is not hypnosis. Even if we go back to that thing we call normal waking consciousness, it would be hard to describe that state as not being hypnosis as well. I am sure that I haven't come close to describing the many faces of hypnosis in this chapter; that would be a daunting feat. But if I have at least caused you to think of hypnosis and all the possibilities differently, then I have achieved my goal for this chapter.

There are only two things that might be argued are not hypnosis. The first is intellectually focused concentration; though even that could be described as hypnosis and one definition of hypnosis is *focused concentration*. Every hypnotist knows how difficult it is to try to work with someone while that person remains in the conscious, intellectual mind. Even that "focused concentration" does not mean that they are not in trance (hypnosis), just not the particular trance that we desire at that moment. In the movie *What the Bleep Do We Know*, quantum physicists said, "*what we think is real may not be real, and what we think is not real may be what is real.*" Aborigines of Australia believe that the dreamtime is what is real and that what others think of as normal consciousness is the dream. Someone may be right.

The second thing that might not be hypnosis is sleep and this one gets a little dicey. While hypnosis is focused on the subconscious mind, in most cases hypnosis seems to need just the smallest amount of the conscious mind around to be effective (barring perhaps a complete bypass of the critical faculty). Does this mean that if we are asleep then no hypnotic effect can occur? I think we know that statement is not completely true. Within this very book I talk about some of the applications of hypnosis and sleep. However, is there a state of sleep where no hypnotic effects will occur? Perhaps, though that would only be likely in a deep delta state and we need more research to determine that for certain.

Chapter 4

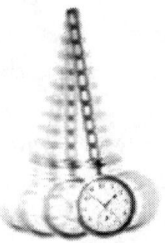

THE FEAR OF HYPNOSIS
(What We Should be Afraid of)

Dr. Graham Wagstaff from the University of Liverpool appeared on the A&E program *The Unexplained*. Dr. Wagstaff, along with Professor Nicolas Spanos of Carleton University in Ottawa Canada, attempt to explain away hypnosis as being nothing out of the ordinary. Spanos does not believe that his subjects go into a "trance," he believes hypnosis has to do with cognitive and social factors. Dr. Wagstaff busies himself putting on demonstrations to disprove the existence of hypnosis or at least to show that it is nothing more than some form of normal consciousness.

There is truth to what these men are saying although I'm not sure that they are aware of it. Hypnosis *is* a normal experience. Dr. Wagstaff goes to great lengths to disprove the phenomenon of hypnosis while using hypnosis the whole time.

Apparently Dr. Wagstaff and Professor Spanos don't possess enough knowledge about hypnosis or trance to understand what they themselves are saying or doing in regard to those subjects.

Why? Why would they even care to go to all of this trouble to be on a television show just to debunk something they don't understand? I guess that statement is its own answer. Because when we fear what we don't understand, we, like Wagstaff and Spanos, try to debunk the phenomenon.

At the end of the show Wagstaff draws the conclusion that none of his subjects were hypnotized and the narrator comments, "Isn't there an easier explanation, maybe they were just hypnotized?" The narrator was correct, the subjects were "just hypnotized," however Wagstaff didn't know enough about hypnosis to realize what he had actually done.

People like this can do more harm than good toward the understanding of hypnosis. When people with doctorates or other distinguished credentials hold forth on subjects about which they are ignorant, the general public may accept what these individuals say, which is a hypnosis of its own (see Waking Hypnosis). It was Wagstaff's and Spanos's fear or lack of understanding that drew them to this program. And, for some viewers, it may have been their own fear about hypnosis that attracted them to watch.

Many people have some fear of hypnosis. When people express a fear of hypnosis, what they are likely expressing is a fear of the unknown. It is my hope that this book will help to alleviate that fear. To say, "I fear hypnosis" is to say, "I fear life," because hypnosis is a continuing part of our daily lives.

In this business of hypnosis we often say that all hypnosis is self hypnosis. Ultimately I believe this statement is true. Certainly, when we have awareness that hypnosis is occurring such as in a clinical setting or when we are performing our own self hypnosis, it is quite true. What about hypnosis that we are not aware of?

The hypnosis that you should be afraid of:

There is hypnosis that we should be afraid of but it is not the hypnosis we get at the hypnotherapist's office or see in a stage show. It's the hypnosis that we aren't even aware of. It's the hypnosis we get from TV and other media. Is it possible that the world is as bad as it looks on the evening news? Go outside and look up and down your street. Is anyone getting shot at out there, is there a tsunami rushing through your neighborhood? Are terrorists kidnapping your family and holding them for ransom? Are aliens landing in your front yard? Is there really all that much to worry about or is the media just profiting from our fears?

Pick up a woman's magazine and look through the ads, and notice how many full page ads there are for pharmaceutical companies. Most of these ads have to do with anti-depressants or some dysfunction that the manufacturers want you to believe can only be alleviated with a simple pill. They don't tell you that adjusting your lifestyle—getting exercise, eating right, changing your thoughts and beliefs—would be a more positive way to get back in balance. Those medications also have negative side effects. Is it possible that pharmaceutical companies and other companies know that by playing into our fears we will buy whatever it is they are selling in order to alleviate that fear?

Advertising and propaganda aren't necessarily bad things. Advertising could be helping us to be aware of products and services that we might not otherwise be aware of or even help us to make better choices. However, the main reason companies and groups are putting out advertising or propaganda is to get us to buy into *their* products or ideals. It may or may not be what we really want or what is best for us. "Choosey mothers choose Jiff." Really? Or do mothers just want to be thought of as choosey? Or do mothers just want to be liked by their children who see Jiff advertised on TV shows? The hypnotic effect of the commercial causes kids to ask mom to buy Jiff. Or what if mothers who were really choosey didn't purchase peanut butter filled with hydrogenated oils, preservatives and sweeteners?

Propaganda and advertising often lie through omission. Manufacturers, politicians, cults, etc. tell us the things we want to hear and not the things that would cause us to think twice. Advertisers tell us all of the benefits we can achieve by using their product while never mentioning that there may be some other cheaper, better way to get the same results.

We all tend to do the same things to some degree. When we are putting out our résumé we include all of the wonderful achievements we have had academically and during our work history. We exclude the part where we majored in panty raids in college, got three women pregnant in Texas, spent some time in jail, or had a DUI.

Do we accept a candidate's political propaganda because we know it is true or because it is what we want to hear? Has anyone ever voted for a candidate because they were going to revise health care or stood for tax reform? Has that ever actually happened or did we just get caught up in the hypnosis of what they were promising? Do you think that anyone has ever voted for a candidate because they were caught up in the hypnosis of being on the same team (Democrat or Republican)? Why isn't there a way to vote against what is being offered without having to vote for something else? Is it possible that drumming the same rhetoric into us is nothing but compounding suggestions until we begin to believe it?

When Ross Perot was running for president a good friend of mine was all excited about everything Perot had to say and was constantly talking about Perot. When it got close to election time I said something to the effect of, "I guess you will finally be getting your chance to vote for Perot." His reply was, "Oh, I'm not going to vote for Perot." I was baffled and asked what he was talking about and he said, "I don't think Perot is going to win so I'm not going to waste my vote on him." I guess it must be more important to be on the winning team than to make a stand for what we believe in. As long as we respond in this manner (buying into the propaganda and wanting to be on the winning team) we will continue to get more of the same.

Our recent president (George W. Bush) used hypnosis to get his way whether he was aware of it or not. I tend to think that he was. Do you recall at all how many times Bush came on TV and used the phrase "weapons of mass destruction?" We heard that phrase over and over again and fear is associated with that phrase. When it came time for Bush to attack Iraq everyone was putty in his hands. We had so much fear as a country that we wanted to get back at the people President Bush told us attacked us. No one really resisted or questioned who or why we were invading another country.

We've seen some really good hypnotists throughout history who we might not think of as such: Hitler, Jesus Christ, Buddha, Jim Jones, religious organizations, governments, educational systems, etc. All use hypnosis techniques to spread their message. While some may think this is negative, and certainly it can be, it can be positive as well. Educational systems promote certain beliefs and even channel students in a certain direction. This could be a beneficial thing or not and that depends on the individual student and his or her learning styles and desires as well.

What about the hypnosis of video games? Kids (and adults) become addicted to these games just like people become addicted to gambling. The little rewards we get by winning a few dollars or moving to the next level keeps a person glued to that screen until, just as they master that game, a new game comes out. Now they can move to an even more lofty level of gaming—all while their studies are being ignored, the lawn is getting longer, and moss and fungus are growing from their unlaundered clothing. Another disturbing thing about these video games is the huge focus on crime and violence. Many games have to do with killing off the enemy one after the other (and by the hundreds) to reach the goal. Some games are based on committing crimes such as stealing cars and then shooting and/or raping people to move to the next level. How might all of this criminal activity in these video games be influencing people in the real world? Could watching these violent games in a trance state actually desensitize these young minds in such a way as to make violent crimes more acceptable to them? Are there any redeeming qualities to video games and is there really any need for video games to be so violent?

There is, of course, the hypnosis of brain washing and mind control that I talk about elsewhere in this book.

This is the hypnosis we need to be concerned about, the hypnosis that we are rarely aware of. The hypnosis that we receive in a therapist's office is not the hypnosis that is likely to create a problem since we are aware and can have control in that situation. It is the hypnosis that creeps in—in ways that we are not always aware of—that should cause us concern.

Chapter 5

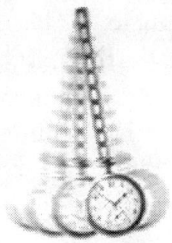

Myths

There are many common myths associated with hypnosis. Most of these myths have formed out of fear due to a lack of understanding about what hypnosis truly is.

Myth #1

Getting stuck in hypnosis:

This myth has most likely arisen from sensations that occur in what is known as the Esdaile state (a hypnotic state where sensations of not being able to move or speak occur). I remember watching a show about hypnosis on TV when I was very young. It must have been around 1953 or 1954. I was quite intrigued by the program and it was well presented, as I recall. As it came to a conclusion, a hypnotist had someone in trance and just as the program ended the hypnotist seemed unable to emerge the subject from hypnosis (for dramatic effect no doubt). This left the audience with an image of the subject helplessly stuck in hypnosis.

While this sort of thing makes good drama for a television show, it also gives the wrong impression to the general public. Yes, there are times when someone in an Esdaile state does not easily emerge from hypnosis, but the person is not trapped at the bottom of his or her subconscious lake struggling to reach the surface, just the opposite. The reason they are not readily emerging is because they don't want to. It feels so good to be in the Esdaile state that they want to stay there and luxuriate in the good feelings. Some hypnotists become concerned when the subject does not return to normal consciousness immediately, but there is no need to worry. The person is not emerging because they don't want to, not because they can't. When emerging someone from an Esdaile state, the therapist has to use an assertive approach that leaves no doubt as to what the outcome will be. If there are any options in the emergence verbiage, other than coming back to normal consciousness, then the subject may become difficult. There are other ways to encourage that person to emerge, however even if nothing was done the person would eventually emerge from hypnosis on his or her own.

Myth #2

The subject will come forth with some hidden secrets:

Some people are afraid that they will blurt out all of their deepest, darkest, most embarrassing secrets in hypnosis. I'm not sure how this myth got started, but it makes me wonder if there aren't a whole lot of people out there with an awful lot of secrets. Is there really that much stuff about everyone that we need to be so secretive about? Or if the rest of the world did know, would anyone really care?

Usually in hypnosis the client isn't speaking unless we are doing an interactive process (when the client and therapist communicate during trance). If the client isn't speaking, how could they possibly reveal anything? Even if we were doing interactive process it doesn't mean the subject is going to go straight to some deep, dark secret and reveal it. The client still has control and if they wouldn't reveal something in their normal, waking state then they won't in hypnosis either.

What if you did reveal some secret? As hypnotists we are obligated by law to make an announcement on the national evening news to let the world know what it was that was said by our client. If anyone from the subject's first grade class to their present day co-workers didn't catch it on the news, it is our job to inform them by courier as to every last detail that was uncovered. I hope you realize that I am saying this with tongue in cheek.

Professional hypnotists have a standard of ethics and practice that we follow which varies from state to state. We are bound by standards of confidentiality and have neither the time nor energy to indulge in unprofessional gossip. If a therapist were to violate confidentiality the client should report that to the therapist's certifying body or to their state government, whichever applies in their locality.

In the state I live in everything is to be held in confidence with some rare exceptions such as child abuse or neglect, or if the client may be in danger (suicide) or a danger to someone else. Everything else is totally confidential unless a release of information is given by the client.

So, no, you won't divulge secrets unless that is what you want to do.

Myth #3

The hypnotist can cause you to do things beyond your control:

I believe that this myth mainly evolved from people watching stage hypnosis shows. Sometimes it does appear as if the hypnotist has total control over the subjects and that is the illusion that the hypnotist wants to create. But is it so?

I was watching a stage hypnotist on a television talk show several years back. I had seen this particular hypnotist on several shows around that time and he was pretty good.

The hypnotist had several hypnotized people on the stage and he was doing different routines with them. At one point he had everyone line up their chairs as though they were going to experience a roller coaster ride. One gentlemen in the group said to the hypnotist, "I can't be on the roller coaster ride!" The hypnotist asked why not, and the man replied, "I have a fear of heights and I don't do roller coaster rides." The hypnotist immediately suggested that the man instead act as the photographer of the event and take pictures of the others riding the coaster. This is what a good hypnotist should do: give everyone a job to do.

The way the whole scene played out was entertaining and did not appear strange to the audience; however underlying that, it did demonstrate that even as much as it appeared that the hypnotist was in control, he could not make a person do something he was not comfortable doing.

Stage hypnotists are working to create the illusion that they are in control and there are things working in their favor to make that possible. Certainly to people in the audience it seems that the hypnotist has people doing things that they (the observers) would never do, and that is probably correct: things that *they would never do*. The hypnotist, however, is skilled at picking out the very kinds of people who *would* do the things that others *would never do* thereby creating an illusion of control and reinforcing the idea that a hypnotist can control others.

Years ago I saw a movie starring Robert Redford called *The Hot Rock*. The movie was about a plan to steal a very precious diamond. At one point the thieves needed to get into a safety deposit box in a bank and they got a woman who was a hypnotist to help them out. She got on an elevator with the bank security person who was going to the vault containing all of the safety deposit boxes. During the elevator ride the hypnotist brought the security person's attention to the display of the changing floor numbers in the elevator and began using this as her induction method (which could actually work). By the time they reached the floor with the safety deposit boxes she had the security person fully hypnotized.

The woman had the guard open a prearranged legitimate safety deposit box. Then she had him remove and unlock a box that was not hers and he did so. While this made for interesting movie going, it simply would not have happened. Someone, especially someone in a position of trust such as this man, would never do anything while hypnotized that would compromise his morals and ethics.

We tell our clients that they are in control and that is true, however it is best for the client to suspend the need to be in control. It's not that the client is giving up control, but rather gaining control in an expanded way. The desired results will occur quickly when the client puts trust in the therapist and allows the therapist to assume leadership in the session.

No hypnotist can make someone do what they don't want to do in a hypnosis session. Ultimately, the client is the one who has the control.

Myth #4

A person will only tell the truth in hypnosis:

Hypnosis is not "truth serum" or a polygraph machine. I have had people bring in their lovers and spouses and ask me to hypnotize them to see if they have been cheating (or for some other purpose) but it is a pointless exercise.

If they've been lying to your face about dropping their pants, then they'll lie to you about it just the same in trance.

One thing is true. In trance, the subconscious mind does not lie. This would seem to mean that someone would not lie in hypnosis; however the conscious mind will always be present enough to take care of all of the lying duties just fine.

It is easy for me to tell if someone is lying simply by the way they speak in hypnosis, though it's not likely that my opinion would mean much in a court of law.

During my work in prisons with several inmates I always knew when they were lying to me in hypnosis (trying to get me to influence the courts no doubt). When I came down on them about it not one of them ever denied that they had tried to pull one over on me.

I have also found it easy to catch people in a lie when using ideomotor signaling (communicating through finger signals and yes or no questions). The subconscious response can come so quickly that the conscious mind doesn't have time to edit the comment. I've had people jump out of trance grabbing at their fingers and saying, "No, I didn't mean that," and I get a good, if private, laugh. But it's too late, they've been had, however I doubt that those ideomotor signals would hold up in court either.

So, no, hypnosis is not a lie detector test.

Myth #5

You will be made to do something against your will:

This myth is a spin off of the myth about being under the control of the hypnotist and likely derives from stage shows and movies.

People think the hypnotist can have a Svengali-like effect, forcing someone to rob a bank and bring the money back. If this were really possible, wouldn't it be happening all the time? Every criminal in town would be coming to me to learn hypnosis if this were true. My wife jokes that if she could get people to do such a thing she wouldn't be wasting her time working so hard.

Hypnotized people can not be made to have sex or to do anything that they wouldn't normally do. It's been tried and tried and tried, and invariably it fails.

A person in hypnosis will not do anything that violates their ethical standards.

Myth #6

The hypnotist will control your mind:

This myth goes along with #3 and #5. Some people think that the hypnotist is going to plant something in your mind or turn you into a zombie or make you quack like a duck or change your political affiliation.

Not so; the client is in control and hypnosis is only occurring because the client is allowing it to occur (self hypnosis).

Myth #7

I can't be hypnotized or only certain kinds of people can be hypnotized:

If you've been reading this book you probably realize that not only *can* everyone be hypnotized, but that everyone *has* been hypnotized. If you think that because you have a high IQ or a strong will that you can't be hypnotized, it is not so. We can make use of your high IQ and strong will to make you a great hypnotic subject.

Hypnotists say that for formal hypnosis to be successful only three things are necessary:

1. An ability to follow simple instructions.
2. A desire to have this change(s) occur/willingness to be hypnotized.
3. An IQ above 70.

I have had some clients that were pushing that 70 IQ mark. That is in no way meant to be demeaning and most of them did quite well. However, we do know that having a high IQ is beneficial for hypnosis. Some early research on that subject is cited in the book *Experimental Hypnosis* by Leslie LeCron.

I have had a few clients that couldn't—or wouldn't—follow instructions and I don't waste my time with them. There is no sense in the therapist getting into a power struggle with the subject. There are other people who need and want our help and would be a better use of energy.

Of course, most people do have a desire to change or they wouldn't be in your office, seeking your services.

If someone doesn't want to be hypnotized then they probably won't be, but why would someone come to a hypnotist's office and pay money only to refuse to be hypnotized?

Some people imagine that they have not been hypnotized when, in fact, they very much were hypnotized. I think some people have such a strong model in their minds of what hypnosis is supposed to be that when they actually experience hypnosis—and it doesn't fit their model—they refuse to believe that they were hypnotized.

Sometimes they will say things like, "I heard every word you said." I guess some people think you are supposed to go deaf when you are being hypnotized. Others might say, "I could have opened my eyes or moved if I wanted to." That's true also; you don't automatically become paralyzed just because you are in hypnosis.

I was at a conference on the west coast several years ago. During a seminar, a well known hypnotist, Gil Boyne, was doing his famous handshake induction routine. He had twenty people on stage and was shaking hands and instantly hypnotizing each individual. One woman in the group said that she hadn't been hypnotized and, in fact, insisted that she is just one of those people who cannot be hypnotized. Gil asked for input from the audience and was rewarded with different characteristics audience members had witnessed about her and just how apparent it was the she had been hypnotized. Even after several people had described her obvious hypnotic state she left the stage still claiming that she had not been hypnotized.

Later I ran into this woman in the lobby of the hotel. I asked if she really thought she hadn't been hypnotized and she replied that she was simply one of those people who could not be hypnotized. I asked her what she did for a living and she said that she was a hypnotherapist. I asked her what kinds of clients she worked with and she said that she specialized in weight loss. I asked her if when she worked with her clients they were in hypnosis. She replied in the affirmative and I continued, "And so do you still think you haven't been hypnotized?" She said, "I am just one of those people who can't be hypnotized." I walked away shaking my head in disbelief. It's one thing to meet someone in the general public who might have such a belief about hypnosis, but not someone who calls herself a hypnotherapist. I hope that particular individual has become better educated by now or perhaps she will come across a copy of this book.

There are certain people who have had a lesion in a particular cortex of the brain who would not do well as hypnotic subjects but this and any other exceptions would be extremely rare.

If you've ever fallen asleep you can be hypnotized.

Yes, you can be hypnotized, if you have any desire to be hypnotized at all.

Myth #8

You will become hypnotized through the power of the hypnotist:

All hypnosis is self hypnosis which means the hypnosis only occurs because the subject allows it to occur. There must be an agreement (consent), whether implied or otherwise, for the hypnosis to occur. Even in a stage show the participants are giving their consent to be hypnotized simply by coming up on stage. I'm sure that in stage hypnosis shows it often appears that the hypnotist has people under his/her power or control, but that is an illusion that any good stage hypnotist creates.

Myth #9

Only weak minded individuals can be hypnotized:

This is totally false and there is research going back to the 1930s (*Experimental Hypnosis*, Le Cron) indicating that having a high intelligence is beneficial to being a good hypnotic subject. It makes sense that someone with high intelligence would have an active imagination and be able to create well in the subconscious mind.

Also: M. M. White in the Journal of Abnormal and Social Psychology, 1930, 25: 293-298.
Davis and Husbands studied this effect using the American Council of Education scholastic aptitude tests.
From Andrew Salter: What is Hypnosis

Myth #10

Hypnosis is Harmful:

It is the unwanted, unrealized hypnosis that we need to be concerned about (see the chapter *Fear of Hypnosis*). In a formal hypnosis session we are completely safe and we may safely assume the hypnotist has our best interest in mind.

In hypnosis the conscious mind maintains some presence—no matter how slight that may be at times—and our moral values and ethics will not be overridden while we are in hypnosis.

Myth #11

Hypnosis is Sleep:

Many people believe that hypnosis is sleep and it is not hard to imagine why. The word hypnosis is Greek for sleep so it is easy to understand that some people might think of it as sleep.

People who are in hypnosis often look as though they are sleeping so it is easy to associate the two things. Oftentimes when someone is hypnotized for the first time they will say, "I just fell asleep" or "It felt like I was sleeping." If you have never been hypnotized before then the closest thing that you can associate to it is sleep, and so it is easy to draw that conclusion.

We can create hypnotic effects when a person is asleep, but for the most part these are two unique and separate realities. To the best of my understanding, to truly be asleep there must be the complete suspension of the conscious mind and I don't believe we will ever get that complete suspension and achieve hypnosis at the same time.

Sometimes even the hypnotist can be fooled and think that the client has fallen asleep; certainly they can appear to be asleep. Usually you find that even in the very deepest states clients will follow simple instructions such as adjusting their breathing upon the hypnotist's suggestion. Sometimes finger movements or other bodily movements can be suggested. However in an Esdaile state the client may well be hypnotized, but won't respond to body movement suggestions.

Myth #12

Hypnotic suggestions last for only a very short time, or they only last for 48 hours:

I am amazed that there are still some hypnotists who believe this. I have heard other hypnotists say that you must get back to their office within 48 hours of your first hypnosis session, so that they can compound the suggestions before they wear off. Again, false.

Salter (*What is Hypnosis*) quoted a piece by Estabrooks recounting a suggestion given to soldiers during WWI that was still effective more than twenty years later. There are also examples of Erickson giving suggestions that lasted more than ten years.

Suggestions that serve a purpose in our lives tend to have a good shelf life, as long as that suggestion is serving us. Suggestions that have no real purpose or meaning for us tend to be short lived. For example, if a stage hypnotist gives you a suggestion that every time the phone rings you will bark like a dog, that may be fun in the moment, but it serves no long-term useful purpose and will shortly disappear. A good stage hypnotist will remove any non-useful suggestions before ending their show, just as a courtesy. The two examples in the preceding paragraph were suggestions given more for entertainment purposes and yet maintained a long shelf life.

Another component impacts the length of a suggestion's duration. Once the subconscious mind has learned a new pattern through suggestion (or any other way) it continues doing the same thing over and over. Now the length of the effectiveness of the suggestion becomes a moot point, since the behavior is likely to continue regardless.

A nice example of this phenomenon is a woman who came to see me not long ago to stop smoking. She had been in to see one of our other therapists almost a year prior. When I asked her what had happened, she said, "Everything was fine for about eight months and then the hypnosis just wore off." I asked her what was going on when she had that first cigarette and she said she was out having drinks with some of her friends and they were smoking and offered her a cigarette, and she decided to try it. I asked how it was. She said it was awful, she said it made her dizzy and nauseous, and she even threw up. I said, "So the hypnosis wore off, huh?" She looked at me like, "oh, well maybe it didn't." I asked her what she thought the hypnosis was supposed to do beyond making her dizzy and sick and vomit? Whether or not the hypnosis wore off is irrelevant because her subconscious had already accepted a new behavior and she had become a non-smoker. The hypnosis was working fine, but I am not sure about the client.

I've heard other somewhat similar comments over the years that go something like this: "I went to a hypnotist to stop smoking and it didn't work." When I question the individual further I find out something like this: "I left the hypnotist's office and I was still smoking, but a few weeks later I just stopped on my own." What people don't often realize is that the hypnotist's suggestions didn't just stop the minute they got up and left the office. For the next few weeks those suggestions continued to grind away in their subconscious until they somehow "magically" ended up no longer smoking. I usually give suggestions like the "No Suggestion Suggestion" (*Power Patter*) that are deliberately meant to continue working on the client's subconscious mind long after they have left my office.

So the conclusion turns out to be variable. The life of a suggestion is not definite; it can have a very long life, but, other than for entertainment purposes, it is never extremely short.

Myth #13

All hypnosis is self hypnosis:

As hypnotists we use this statement over and over and essentially it is true; however a more accurate rendering might be: All formal hypnosis is self hypnosis. There is hypnosis that occurs that we are not always aware of, and we are not controlling it, and it does have an effect on us. Television, advertising, politics, video games create a hypnosis as well. We aren't aware of it and therefore we are influenced to some extent beyond our control (see the chapter *Fear of Hypnosis*).

The hypnosis that we are aware of is self hypnosis whether we are performing it on ourselves (autohypnosis) or with a facilitator (hetero-hypnosis). The hypnosis that we are aware of is self hypnosis because we are allowing it to occur and have control over it. It seems strange that it is the formal hypnosis that most people are concerned about, even though that is the hypnosis that is most likely to have a positive effect upon us.

Other forms of hypnosis such as daydreaming, staring off into space or staring at a flame are self hypnosis as well (even though we may not be aware of it). These forms of hypnosis are likely to have a positive effect upon us also.

So all formal hypnosis is self hypnosis.

Chapter 6

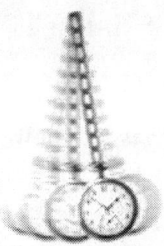

WHAT IS WAKING HYPNOSIS?

I am still somewhat dominated by that feeling of surprise which seized me at my first contact with the American people. In fact, my wonderment has grown every day with the realization of ideas which many people seem to have formed of me and my powers. I do not want people to have a sort of fanatical belief in me. It is true, of course, that blind faith is an asset in favor of a sick person's chances of getting well. People who come to me with the belief already established in their minds that they are going to be cured are more than half way on the road to recovery before they see me.

—*Emile Coué*
My Method, Page 82

Waking hypnosis as defined by Dave Elman in his classic book *Hypnotherapy* is as follows: "When hypnotic effects are achieved without the use of the trance state, such hypnotic effects are called waking hypnosis. In every case, it involves a bypass of the critical faculty and the implanting of selective thinking." Elman goes on to explain how waking hypnosis, or waking suggestion, has been used to perform surgeries and painless dentistry.

The bypass of the critical faculty is a <u>very</u> high form of hypnosis and may be the most profound use and example of hypnosis there is. I don't know that Elman ever totally defined what that bypass of the critical faculty meant to him in terms of waking hypnosis, and I don't know if he believed that all hypnosis meant a total bypass of the critical faculty or if we might achieve some sort of partial bypass of the critical faculty. Some of his other references to the bypass lead me to believe that either he believed there was always a total bypass of the critical faculty when hypnosis occurred, or he used that verbiage regardless of whether it was a complete or partial bypass of the critical faculty.

While referring to waking suggestion, however, Elman did refer to waking suggestion as not needing the bypass of the critical faculty. To quote Elman directly, "A waking suggestion is a suggestion given in a normal state of consciousness which does not precipitate a waking state of hypnosis." He went on to use the example of when one person in a group begins to yawn (non-verbal suggestion), others will begin to yawn as well, which is a good example of hypnosis.

In my opinion and observation, the bypass of the critical faculty can occur in degrees. For instance, when I'm working with someone and they are in a lighter trance, such as an Alpha state, there is what I would call a softening of the critical faculty which causes the subconscious mind to be more available to the positive suggestions that I am giving. In a deeper state, such as in Theta or at the level we refer to as Somnambulism, that softening effect is even more profound and the suggestions are even more likely to have a positive effect on the subconscious mind. That is to say that, during normal suggestion work, we do not have a total bypass of the critical factor yet could achieve that total bypass at least at times.

Often the total bypass of the critical faculty is a very brief window that a hypnotist can take advantage of if they are aware of the opening. For instance, when we use instant inductions we are getting a complete bypass of the critical faculty in order to get the client into hypnosis instantly.

Often that bypass is caused by misdirection. Misdirection occurs when the mind is expecting one thing to occur and then something radically different occurs. In that moment, when the mind is unable to make sense of what is going on (or what is happening in the moment doesn't fit into normal paradigms), the hypnotist has a brief window of opportunity to have a suggestion immediately accepted. The normal suggestion (or command) that is given during that window of opportunity is "**sleep!**" Since in that brief moment the mind does not know what else to do, it goes along with the one suggestion that it does know how to do. The hypnotist will then need to continue giving the subconscious some direction at that point so that the trance state will continue. There is no doubt that the subject will go straight into a somnambulistic state the moment that the "**sleep!**" command is given.

We can gain that bypass of the critical faculty when the client is already in trance as well. Sometimes the hypnotist will again use misdirection or confusion to gain the bypass of the critical faculty.

While the bypass of the critical faculty may represent a very profound example of waking hypnosis (and of hypnosis itself) it is only one form of waking hypnosis.

Melvin Powers talks about waking hypnosis in his book *Advanced Techniques of Hypnosis*. He refers to the use of waking hypnosis as it is used in medical and dental situations (which might well be using the bypass of the critical faculty) and even cites a book entitled *Suggestion* written by George C Pitzer, M.D. *Suggestion* was written in 1889 about Pitzer's experiences with waking hypnosis (so this has been known and used for some time). Many applications of medical hypnosis use the placebo effect or the "sterile syringe," as it was sometimes referred to. The placebo effect is hypnosis, and I will explain that more in depth in its own chapter.

Mr. Powers continues discussing the other applications of waking hypnosis and refers to its use through propaganda and advertising. We often talk about the use of hypnotic languaging and suggestion in advertising, and especially on television. Mr. Powers refers to hypnosis in television advertising and I find that quite interesting since his book was published in 1953. I was around in 1953 and there wasn't a lot of anything on TV in 1953, yet the use of hypnosis was already well established according to Powers (whether or not the advertisers were aware of it).

Certainly when we, as hypnotists, perform imagination exercises, (suggestibility tests) waking hypnosis is being applied. These imagination exercises are methods that we use (individually or in groups) to determine someone's ability to be hypnotized or, more accurately, to accept suggestion. Some people are more responsive than others. In his book *New Master Course in Hypnotism* (1948) author Harry Arons expands on this and explains how to take the exercises even further by using them to take the individual into somnambulism.

While all of these examples of waking hypnosis are valid, none of them really give us a glimpse into the true breadth and depth of what waking hypnosis is. In fact, waking hypnosis is so much a part of our existence that we are oblivious to its impact and how to take advantage of it. Every one of us is using or is being influenced by waking hypnosis constantly.

I lecture my students on the importance of understanding waking hypnosis and its importance to what we do. I tell them that if we are good at the waking hypnosis, then once we get the client into formal hypnosis, we could read to them from the phone book and achieve the desired results.

Expectancy is hypnosis. When we expect that a certain outcome will occur, that is what tends to occur. When we create the expectancy in the waking hypnosis that a particular outcome will occur as a result of what we do here today, then that is what tends to occur. Let's say that someone comes into my office and wants to stop smoking. During that individual's pre-talk I will convince him/her that he/she will be leaving my office as a non-smoker for the rest of his/her life. Once we have created that expectancy in the client's mind, the client leaves his/her session as a non-smoker for the rest of his/her life. The success of the hypnosis session can depend very heavily on waking hypnosis (creating expectation in the client).

Paradigms (models that we operate within) have a lot to do with our expectancy and the critical faculty as well. We all operate within a set of beliefs and those beliefs help to create the expectations (waking hypnosis) of our daily lives. If I have certain beliefs or assumptions about how the world works (expectancy) then that is how the world tends to work for me. If I am a pickpocket, I might view the world around me as an opportunity to find an easy mark. The police officer might walk down the street viewing everyone as a possible criminal. The evangelist might see everyone as someone to convert. These paradigms that we operate within color (hypnotize) our experience of the world around us. See my book *The Power of the Past* for more on this topic.

Our religious, political and educational backgrounds (and more) all play into our paradigms and therefore into the waking hypnosis that is associated with those things. I have had the opportunity of late to be around some Hassidic Jews. Their dedication to their belief system is inspiring and the waking hypnosis created by that must affect their every thought. The more dedicated we are to one of these belief systems, the more the waking hypnosis around that system influences our every thought and movement. That is not to say that a religious or political belief or work ethic, etc. is right or wrong, but simply that it creates a unique waking hypnosis.

Many years ago it was believed that the world was flat, and in one respect it was. Not because of actual topography, of course, but because people were living (restricting their lives) as if it were a flat world. People limited themselves based on flat world (waking hypnosis) limitations. How many ways is the waking hypnosis that we have created through our belief systems affecting us? Are those beliefs systems (waking hypnosis) correct? Are they good, bad, or indifferent

While the words a hypnotist uses are the most powerful tools that he/she possesses, these words are not our only options. Certainly we can help to create waking hypnosis through our advertising, such as in our brochures, Yellow Pages ads, internet sites, newspaper ads, signage or business cards.

Presentation is also very important. A therapist may work out of the basement of his/her home; however, to the prospective client, that environment does not shout out, "Successful, professional, therapist!" It creates a waking hypnosis, but not the waking hypnosis we want. When a client walks into one of our clinics, they come into a professional, well managed facility. They are greeted by a receptionist and made to feel comfortable. The offices reflect a professional, business like feel. That does not mean that you need to be sterile or impersonal; in fact, it is good to personalize your office. Just don't allow that to become the consuming message about you. Having some pieces of art is fine, but keep in mind that something you may find quite appealing may be distracting to others. No matter how you decorate your office you are creating a waking hypnosis; it's a matter of what kind of waking hypnosis you want to create. You may feel that you have a knack for such things, but also allow for some creative input.

Part of your presentation and the waking hypnosis is your own appearance. Wearing long, flowing robes, dripping with crystals, with incense burning near your crystal ball, and sitar music playing in the background may work if your office is in the back of a metaphysical bookstore. It would however seem very unprofessional to most clients. Dressing professionally is important and that varies depending on where you are or what you are doing. Wearing cowboy boots might work fine in Austin, but not in Boston. Wearing a suit and tie can work well in some atmospheres, especially if the one wearing the suit is trying to gain an advantage in terms of power differential to negotiate business. In a hypnosis practice we want to stay professional, but not appear ridged or severe. Most of our clients are already dealing with stress, and a button down shirt with a coat and tie does not say to anyone, "relax," or "I am approachable." It can be easier to just throw on a coat and tie, but is that really the waking hypnosis we want to create? I want my clients to feel at ease and be able to really relax.

Similarly, if you are talking to your clients from behind a desk you are creating a power differential which might work well for business dealings, but not for successful therapy. No matter what type of business you are in, it is necessary to look at the presentation you are communicating (waking hypnosis).

If someone comes to me and they want to lose weight and I weigh 350 lbs, what is the waking hypnosis that I am creating? Believability is part of the waking hypnosis. If who I am is not believable what is the waking hypnosis I am creating?

Demeanor is also part of the waking hypnosis. Your very actions, the way you carry yourself and act, are all part of the waking hypnosis. Have you ever watched a comedian walk out on stage and go up to the microphone and not say a thing, yet the audience breaks out into laughter? This is waking hypnosis. The comedian, for what ever reason, whether it is through his presentation, demeanor, or the expectancy that he has created, has caused anything he does (even nothing) to be funny. This is his waking hypnosis. "Heeeeers Johnny" is a statement that Ed McMahon used before Johnny Carson walked out on stage. "Heeeeers Johnny" became a hypnotic suggestion, creating expectancy in the audience that something funny was about to occur because that is what the audience had come to expect. As a result, Johnny might not have been on the top of his game some nights, but people were already on the edge of their seats with anticipation and expectation.

Your doctor (or any professional) is using waking hypnosis, whether or not he/she means to, and that waking hypnosis can work for or against him/her. The way the individual dresses, acts, talks, even the diplomas on the wall, create the waking hypnosis. Someone in a position of authority has more power to create waking hypnosis than your spouse or brother in-law. When the doctor tells you to go on a diet, it's likely to make a bigger impact than if your wife suggested the same thing. Going on a diet is just as important to our well being, no matter who suggests it, but when it's the doctor who suggests it, we give it greater respect. On the other hand, if that same doctor tells you that you only have six weeks to live, that statement will have a greater impact, even if it is not correct. Depending on how that suggestion is given, it can become even more effective. If the doctor has just gotten your tests back from the lab and says to you "you have cancer!" the moment he makes the statement, "you have cancer" he has just gotten the bypass of the critical faculty and the next thing he says will have a clear path straight into your subconscious mind. If his next words are "you have six weeks to live," then you have just been given a very powerful suggestion (even if it is not correct) and that suggestion will have a profound effect.

Doctors, or any others in a position of power, will have easier access to the subconscious mind simply because of their position or status. This means that their suggestions will be more readily received, and that they will be more able to achieve the bypass of the critical faculty.

I had been working with a woman for weight loss and she was responding quite well and experiencing good results. She showed up one morning an hour early for her session. Since I wasn't in yet she walked into the doctor's office on the first level of my building and asked the doctor if he knew when I would be in. He said he didn't know and asked why she was seeing me. When she told him that she was seeing me for weight loss, he responded with, "well, I do hypnosis as well and it doesn't work for weight loss."

Obviously this doctor did not know much about hypnosis or he wouldn't have made that statement. Now I was left with the task of getting my client back on track after this doctor had just sabotaged the good progress she was making. Simply because he was a doctor that placed him a position of authority and knowledge (waking hypnosis) which gave him the ability to override what we had accomplished. No matter how good a doctor he might have been, his scant knowledge of hypnosis was just enough to cause problems, but not enough to help anyone with weight issues.

Some doctors will talk negatively about hypnosis. If they actually understood what hypnosis is and what it can do they would likely respond differently. The truth is hypnosis is a huge part of doctors' lives, whether or not they know it. If they understood it better they could make use of it to their own advantage, even simply in the waking hypnosis of their daily practice.

It is very important that we are aware of what we say and do. It is even more important that people in a position of power, or perceived power, be more aware.

My wife, Lynsi, and I practice a certain style of yoga fairly regularly. Being hypnotists, we are quite aware of people's language and the effect that they are having on others. Anyone who is in front of a group of people is perceived to be in a position of authority, no matter how real that might be. There is a very slender young man who instructs some of the classes. He is a good instructor; however he has often made references to how he likes doing the yoga so that he can go to Burger King and eat a whopper and fries without feeling guilty. Many people who are coming to yoga classes are trying to get a better grip on their lifestyle choices and this young man in front of the group suggesting that burgers and fries could somehow be okay for them is not helping the situation at all. Initially, this young man's waking hypnosis is good because he is lean and healthy-appearing, but then he undermines the good hypnosis with suggestions of junk food.

Whenever someone is leading a group there will be a good amount of waking hypnosis occurring (like the comedian example and the yoga instructor). If someone is giving a talk on a particular subject, it doesn't matter how much they know if they come across with a lack of confidence or are unsure of themselves. On the other hand, some people possess the charisma to command attention from a group, no matter what they might be talking about. I have gone to several talks given by Wayne Dyer or Deepak Chopra. These speakers have a really good waking hypnosis working for them. They have created a certain expectancy about how the evening will go and that is the way it goes. Even people who have not been to one of their talks have probably seen them on TV and so a certain expectancy has been created. I would guess that no matter what location or period of time one of their talks occurs, a similar audience response and experience would be the result.

I was at a day long conference at Boecher Hall, in Denver, back in the seventies, where several well known speakers had come to talk. One talk that I really enjoyed that day was by the late Buckminster Fuller. His presentation was followed by the psychic Jean Dixon. I didn't know a lot about Jean Dixon, although I knew she made predictions about the future and that she had a newspaper column. It was an election year and I believe Ronald Reagan was running for president. When Jean came out she started talking about the election and her opinions about Ronald Reagan. Whatever her opinions were on the matter she had the wrong audience and things started to become confrontational. I would have to guess that this wasn't the first time she had ever spoken in front of a group, and that she would know to stick to the topic that she was there for, but no, she was going to poke a sleeping lion with a stick just to see if it was hungry or not.

Soon the entire audience was grumbling and even those people who might have shared her political views wanted her to shut up. She wasn't sensitive enough to see where she was headed and shift directions to salvage her talk. She had inadvertently created a waking hypnosis (mob mentality) that she didn't know how to handle. Someone yelled an angry comment out to her and she replied, "Well, then who should be president?" In that moment I yelled out at the top of my lungs, "Donald Duck!" The whole place just cracked up laughing. I had gotten the bypass of the critical faculty on two thousand people in an instant, and the energy in the room shifted just that quickly. Because everyone's mood and energy was heading in one direction and because my suggestion was so absurd (misdirection) I was able to get the bypass of the critical faculty (shifting the waking hypnosis) and everyone saw just how ridiculous the situation had become. (And a lynching was avoided.) Personally, I would have voted for Donald Duck, at least I believe he's an independent.

After my waking hypnosis Jean was able to get back on track and make it through the rest of her talk. She has never earned my respect, however if she was still around she would owe me a dinner and that might help.

I don't know how confident Jean was, but she must have had a certain amount of confidence just to get up in front of all of those people. Confidence plays a huge role in waking hypnosis. If I am confident as a hypnotist and I am confident that I can help someone, then that makes them more confident that we will achieve their goal and therefore our desired result is the result that occurs.

Confidence is hypnosis; confidence is both verbal and non-verbal suggestion. I am creating a positive waking hypnosis when I speak (give suggestions) in a confident manner. Our very demeanor, how we act and look and move, can give an air of confidence (waking hypnosis). I tell my students over and over, "Be confident. If you don't feel confident then act like you are confident, fake it till you make it." Be an actor, actors become the person, the mood they are playing, they feel the emotions. The more you act confident the more confident you will become. The more you practice your trade, the more skill you achieve and the more confident you will naturally be.

Speak as if the desired results are a forgone conclusion. If success is the only option available then that will be the outcome. If I told smokers that there is a pretty good chance that they could leave my office a non-smoker, I would be leaving opportunity for failure to occur. However, no matter what doubts my clients might have, I counter them with the assurance that they will walk out that door a non-smoker for the rest of their lives.

Parents have been using waking hypnosis (suggestion) forever. Let's say that dad leaves town from time to time on business. Dad has a business conference to attend next month in Miami. Mom and dad decide that this business trip would be a great opportunity for them to extend into a getaway for some alone time. Once the decision has been made, they begin telling little Billy and little Sally how mom and dad have to leave town for business and how they are going to get to stay at the farm with Uncle Tom and Aunt Sue and play with their cousins for a week. They remind the kids several times about what a great time they will have staying on the farm while dad and mom take care of business. The parents are creating an expectancy (waking hypnosis) that will work in their favor. When the time arrives, the kids head off to the farm with excited anticipation of what the week away will be like and all goes well. Parents can and do create a waking hypnosis in this kind of situation that causes the opposite effect by saying, "Dad and I are going to have to leave town on business and we know you will be missing us a lot and you will probably cry, but hopefully your aunt Sue can make it better."

Parents are also using waking hypnosis on children through their body language. Arms folded across the chest may be enough to get a child's attention. Combine those folded arms with a raised eyebrow, or clearing of the throat or a tapping foot (non-verbal suggestions) and the fear of God causes the child to straighten up. Because those body postures are associated with something else (anchors and triggers), like a spanking or time out, they impact junior in an advantageous manner. There is an in depth explanation on the use of anchors and triggers in my book *The Power of the Past*. Also see conditioned response in this book.

Group waking hypnosis can occur in many ways. Have you ever been in a meeting or class where one person in the room comments on the room temperature (a waking suggestion), which brings other people's attention to the room temperature, and then perhaps someone else agrees (compounding suggestions)? Pretty soon everyone in the room is focused on the temperature to the point of disrupting the meeting. Eventually the custodian is brought in and says everything is working just fine and even adjusts the temperature; or maybe the meeting ends up moving to another room. If you ever want to disrupt a meeting, just keep questioning the temperature in the room.

I have a little routine that I do when I'm talking to my classes about suggestibility testing or if I'm giving a talk somewhere. I bring a fresh lemon and I begin cutting it in half so that everyone can plainly see what I am doing. Then I take a big bite out of that lemon while everyone is watching. People in the audience grimace and their mouths pucker up and salivate just from watching me bite into the lemon (non-verbal suggestion). This is another group waking hypnosis. Everyone responds to this demonstration, some more so than others. The more someone responds to this demonstration, the more likely they are to be a good candidate for other demonstrations that I will be doing. If I didn't have a lemon with me I could just talk about the lemon and biting into it and that would be enough to cause a reaction from the audience.

I can do a similar thing with story telling. If I am good at telling a story, I can cause physical and emotional changes to occur within the audience no matter how large or small that audience might be.

In fact, not long ago, I was driving back to town on a dark country road and my headlights were the only light available. Up ahead in my lights I could see a puppy along side the road that had obviously been hit by a passing motorist. The puppy was struggling to get up, but its rear legs looked as though they had been paralyzed. Being an animal lover all sorts of thoughts were running through my mind. There were no farmhouses nearby where I could go to ask for help or find out where the puppy might belong. Perhaps someone had thoughtlessly dumped it to fend for itself. I wondered about where the closest all night veterinary clinic might be. I didn't even have a cell phone to call and find out if there were any emergency services near by. I have had to put animals out of their misery before because they were too far gone, but I didn't have a gun handy.

As I got closer and closer to the little puppy I became more and more concerned. Perhaps the puppy had a collar and a name tag and that would help me to find its owners. As I got right up to the suffering puppy and slowed to a stop it was plain to see in my head lights that the injured puppy was nothing but a brown paper bag that had become stuck in the mud by the edge of the road and the wind was giving it life. It was only my own imagination that caused it to become an injured puppy. My own imagination had created a waking hypnosis that brought up all sorts of feelings in me (and now you), and while the feelings and hypnosis were real, the puppy was only a paper bag.

A group waking hypnosis occurs when we are at the movie theatre as well. The actors on the movie screen are creating all sorts of different emotional responses in the crowd through two dimensional images and analog sound.

Who hasn't found themselves leaving a movie feeling inspired, or full of joy, or sobbing?

I was involved in a great example of group waking hypnosis many years ago when I attended the *Fire Walk Experience* with Tony Robbins. I knew when I walked into the large hotel conference room that I was ready to do the fire-walk that very minute. I knew that hypnotically I had already prepared myself and was ready to go. However there were three hundred other people in the conference room who weren't yet properly hypnotized to perform the amazing feat.

We went through a lengthy ceremony (hypnosis) that prepared the audience to walk barefoot on hot coals. The ceremony included various exercises we performed, listening to rock music, as well as the whole group going out into a parking lot and watching the wood being laid out in a pit and set on fire. There was a lot of talk about previous experiences that people had had walking on hot coals. The last thing that we did before actually walking on the coals was to watch Tony Robbins walk through the coals first. One after the other, we all walked successfully across the coals (a few people may have chosen not to) and no one experienced any burns or blisters. This *Fire Walk Experience* is based on the Kajunas. The Kajunas were known for doing a fire walk which followed several days of ritual. Tony Robbins had cut the several days of ritual down to an evening of ritual. The evening of ritual leading up to the fire walk amounts to nothing but waking hypnosis and waking suggestions that create the expectation (hypnosis) that we will successfully walk across hot coals with no negative results.

What about even larger group hypnosis? How big could it get? Each state, country, and continent has a waking hypnosis connected to it. We in the USA have a certain waking hypnosis that may reflect our abundant lifestyle and our somewhat rebellious nature. We think and talk about ourselves being American to the point that we exclude Canada, Mexico, and all of the South American countries, when we use the term American.

Norsemen or the Huns have a waking hypnosis surrounding them of being very strong and tough, and rightfully so. Just their potential presence had a certain waking hypnosis connected with it. We stereotypically believe that every Asian is smart and certainly a mathematical genius, yet somehow can't drive a car. An Asian comedian I once saw on TV said that he was not a good Asian. He said he even flunked math class and that when he flunked, five white kids around him flunked too.

When a nation heavily identifies itself with a religious or political system, there is a hypnosis associated with that. Socialists may see themselves much differently than we see them in the USA. We all like to believe that our King, Queen, Chief, President or Dictator is the best there is.

Other group waking hypnosis occurred in this country during the days of the cold war with Russia. Whether there was any real threat of war or not, we lived our lives with a cloud of threat hanging over us every minute of our existence. During the time of the Great Depression another waking hypnosis was occurring. Few of the people that were present during that era are even around now, yet the mentality of scarcity (hypnosis) that was created during that time was passed down to many of us and is still alive and well, even though the conditions that created it are long gone.

One morning I got up to go to work and turned on the TV. Katie Couric was interviewing a man on the streets of New York. As they looked up into the sky, the man explained how he had seen a small plane crash into one of the twin towers. It was September 11, 2001. Huge group hypnosis was occurring on that day in September. The man being interviewed had his own waking hypnosis occurring at that moment. Even though he saw the plane crash into the first tower his mind could not get wrapped around anything but a small plane doing such a thing. His paradigms of how the world is supposed to work did not include airliners crashing into sky scrapers. While he continued to describe what he had seen an airliner crashed into the second tower. Now many paradigms were being challenged.

Certainly a mass hypnosis took place on that September morning and that hypnosis has continued to some degree ever since. We will not be traveling again soon without feeling the effects of that morning. An economical hypnosis occurred as well. Some businesses ended as a result, and we certainly felt the effects.

What effect does the media have on the group waking hypnosis? I believe the media has a tremendous power in shaping beliefs and emotions. How much compounding of our anxiety did seeing the twin towers coming down over and over again have on us? A recent article in *Psychology Today* said that, due to the fear associated with 9/11, 1,000 people in this country died simply because they chose to drive on their vacations instead of fly. How many of them would still be alive if they hadn't been bombarded with the constant fear that was generated by the press?

John Stausall did a TV story a year or two ago. He reported how we are now in the safest period of history we have ever been in, but we believe ourselves to be in the least safe time ever. I would have to give a lot of the credit for that to the media. Whenever we turn on the news or open a newspaper what is it that we see? The front page or opening news story is not about a kitten being rescued from a tree. The news focuses on whatever disaster is occurring in the world. As a result, the average person feels like there is a mass murderer or a tsunami waiting for them in the front yard.

If a hurricane had hit New Orleans a hundred and fifty years ago, who would have known? By the time we finally got that information it would have been months later and too late to do anything about it. Nowadays if Prince Harry gets bitten by a mosquito while on maneuvers it creates front page news all over the world.

Several years ago there were freeway killings back east. A news story came on while Lynsi and I were watching TV. They were reporting on how they were looking for a white van which had been spotted at the shootings several times. I said to Lynsi, "It's hypnosis." She said, "What are you talking about?" I told her there is no white van. Everyone is so focused on a white van that it has created a hypnosis around white vans. I said, "Go to any shopping mall in this country and show me one that doesn't have white vans in it. The country has become so focused on there being a white van that they don't realize that there is no white van." And, sure enough, it was a wild goose chase because the killers weren't using a white van. The media had helped to create this hypnosis and fear. Sure, people will argue that we need to know what is going on in the world, and to some extent we do, but at some point enough is enough.

If the media has a prejudice toward a certain idea or political candidate then they can create a hypnosis in favor of their ideals. In countries where the press is controlled by the government the authorities will create the hypnosis that works in their favor.

A group (or individual) waking hypnosis can occur at a party or similar type of gathering. If someone starts passing the word through the crowd that the punch has been heavily spiked with Everclear people will begin to act silly—giggling, and saying and doing ridiculous things.

Another waking hypnosis occurs around school and test taking. If we assume that a certain instructor is tough or a hard grader, that is what happens. When we expect that the upcoming exam or finals are going to be tough, that becomes a self-fulfilling prophecy (hypnosis).

A certain mystique has been created around the bar exam that law students must pass in order to practice law. The statistics for passing the bar exam indicate that few will pass it on their first attempt, a fact that the students have been made well aware of all through law school. A waking hypnosis has been created which is working against the law students. I have worked with many of these individuals. It doesn't take a lot to determine that they are intelligent and know their profession, and that they have all of the information they need to pass the exam, yet they have become convinced that this bar exam is some sort of a monster.

Earlier in this chapter I talked about the office setting and how that plays into the whole waking hypnosis experience. That is true for other settings as well. Some businesses go to great lengths to choose colors and décor that will have a beneficial effect on their patrons. Certain colors will have relaxing or activating effects. In a spa you want an effect that will allow people to slow down and relax, but in another environment you might want the décor to encourage expedience and high-volume turnover.

Perhaps you have walked into a place of worship and felt a sense of awe. Taking in the Sistine Chapel has a much different waking hypnosis connected to it than going into your fourteen year old's bedroom. People in these experiences have a waking hypnosis connected to them as well. Notice how you feel in the presence of a monk or a priest compared to that fourteen year old. And this is true for lots of people we come into contact with. Having a meeting with the president of your college or CEO of your company has a much different waking hypnosis connected to it than dropping a quarter in the hat of some homeless person.

The waking hypnosis created at an athletic competition can vary widely, depending on the teams or competitors and how fierce the competition gets. Whether your team or the competitor is winning or losing can create an entirely different waking hypnosis. There is a lot of waking hypnosis occurring at the Super Bowl, even after the competition is over. For days after there can be a waking hypnosis throughout the country, particularly in the home towns and states of the participating teams. The winning towns and states are experiencing a much different waking hypnosis than those in the losing regions. Both sides have experienced the waking hypnosis that comes with overindulging in beer and pizza, and chips and salsa.

The waking hypnosis attached to a rally can vary widely. We can be rallying behind our candidate for class president at our local high school, or rallying to overthrow the government.

If you get into a car that is clean and neat and well kept you will tend to conduct yourself differently than you would in an unwashed vehicle that is strewn with fast food wrappers and cigarette butts.

The waking hypnosis changes depending on our surroundings, who we might be with, and what the situation is at the moment. The waking hypnosis that one experiences while driving in a Lamborghini Macielago is considerably different from the hypnosis attached to driving a Yugo. We feel much different, and relate to the world differently, while wearing an Armani suit than we do when dressed in greasy overalls.

The hypnosis associated with living in a luxurious palace is much different than that created by living under a bridge and sleeping in a cardboard box.

Our manners and demeanor change depending on the waking hypnosis of the moment. Wiping your mouth with your shirt sleeve while sitting in front of a camp fire is one thing. Having dinner at the White House produces a different set of social behaviors altogether.

Waking Hypnosis and Dentistry:

Lots of dentists have had some exposure to hypnosis. Some dentists have a great deal of expertise in using hypnosis and others may have had no more than a brief course or a lecture on hypnosis as part of their training. Prior to the development of modern anesthetics, hypnosis was more widely used in dentistry. While we think of hypnosis as an anesthetic, it also has many other practical purposes for dentists. Many patients have fears and anxiety around going to the dentist, and hypnosis can be very effective at making these trips to the dentist more comfortable. Dentists would do well to continue using hypnosis, if only in the waking portion that helps to alleviate fears.

Several years ago I went to my dentist to have a tooth extracted. The dentist I was seeing at the time had some training in hypnosis as part of his normal schooling, and was supportive of its use, even though he had not made much use of it in his practice. However I did notice that his waking hypnosis was quite good, whether he was aware of it or not. One of the things that he did well was to keep the syringe out of my field of vision. He was very skilled at moving around and injecting Novocain into those areas that needed to be deadened without allowing me to see the syringe. After the procedure was complete and I was leaving the examining room, I saw the syringe with its ten inch long needle lying on an instrument tray. I thought to myself at that moment that he had done a great job with the waking hypnosis.

That long syringe is by itself a kind of waking hypnosis. Any length of needle would be capable of injecting enough anesthetic to do the job. The long needle is only to help get to those hard to reach areas. However there is something about that long needle that gets to us psychologically, much like staring down the end of a double barrel 12 gauge shotgun gets our attention. A 22 caliber pistol would kill you just as dead, but seeing those big, round openings in our face demands a respect that a 22 will never achieve.

More recently I found myself visiting a dental surgeon for a more difficult type of extraction. Although I'm sure he was very knowledgeable about dental surgery, his waking hypnosis could use some improvement. He said that I would need someone to drive me home after the procedure since he was going to use a general anesthetic. I said I did not have someone to drive me home and that he would just have to do the procedure without a general anesthetic. He asked me if I was some sort of masochist (waking hypnosis) or what? He said he had never done this procedure without a general anesthetic, (again, thank you very much for the waking hypnosis) but he went ahead any way. I rejected all of his negative suggestions because in my mind I knew I could override it with my own hypnosis. While waiting in the chair for him to get started, I did my own self hypnosis. I left feeling fine and got on a plane for the east coast the next morning with no difficulties whatsoever.

Counter Waking Hypnosis:

There is a variation on waking hypnosis that I would refer to as a "counter waking hypnosis." This is an unwanted hypnotic effect that can occur following a client's session.

Let's say that I have successfully worked with a client for fear of flying and now they are ready to get on a plane and go somewhere. The only problem is that they won't be traveling anywhere for the next three months. This in itself is not the problem. The problem arises when other people close to this person (friends and family) have shared in the clients issue around flying. Now the client is free of the fear of flying, however, the people around him are still caught up in the old hypnosis and they haven't changed. In fact, there may even be a benefit for them in the client's maintaining the unwanted behavior.

Since there is a good deal of time before my client's next flight, there is also a good deal of opportunity for some well meaning friend or family member to screw it up. Even though the client has experienced the positive results that he came in for, there is time for someone to create doubt in his mind. Someone may say something like, "I'll bet you're really dreading that flight to Boston in May, remember how terrifying that last flight you took was?" or "Hypnosis! What are you thinking? That is never going to work, you just wasted your money" or "You need to be renewing your prescription for Xanax so you can at least tolerate that flight."

These kinds of suggestions (counter suggestions) place doubt in the client's mind and can retrigger those old feelings and sensations around the unwanted behavior (waking hypnosis). This is one reason why I get clients to test out the hypnosis right away. If they are getting on a plane that same afternoon and all goes well it will be unlikely that some uncaring or insensitive individual will have a chance to override the good work that has been done. The counter suggestion, even though it has been given in a "normal waking state," has a lot of hypnotic power associated with it. Since there is a good deal of emotion (terror occurred before) and logic (past history of this negative experience that is hard to deny) associated with it, a counter suggestion could even get a bypass of the critical faculty.

So, while waking hypnosis does include the bypass of the critical faculty as Elman referred to, it is only a glimpse at one part of a very large elephant. Atmosphere, ambience, attitude, expectancy and paradigms are also big contributors to waking hypnosis. And, of course, that pesky little demon *the placebo* is another variant of waking hypnosis.

Chapter 7

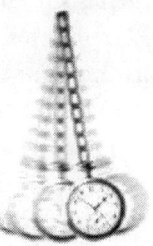

THE PLACEBO EFFECT

It is sufficient to think: I am constipated to become constipated! It is the idea that we have that unless we take such and such a medicine, we shall not have an evacuation of the bowels every day. It is true, for if someone were to introduce surreptitiously into your box of pills or cachets, cachets containing starch or bread pills, having the identical outward appearance of your usual cachets or pills, your bowels would work in exactly the same manner as if you had taken your pill of extract of rhubarb, or a cachet containing cascara! But of course, only on the condition that you knew nothing whatever about it! It is the same with those injections of distilled water that they give to patients, telling them that they are injections of morphia! They believe that it is morphia and they feel relieved!

Emile Coué
How to Practice Suggestion and Autosuggestion
Page 60

A good friend, colleague, and former student of mine, Greig (Greg) Thomson told me this story. Years ago Greig was an engineer at General Electric. Greig's young daughter had been having issues with warts on her hands. One evening when Greig arrived home from work he had a mysterious vial with him. He explained to his daughter that this vial contained some top secret atomic water that they had been developing at General Electric. He told his daughter of the amazing healing powers that had been discovered in this atomic water and how he had managed to smuggle some of it out.

Greig applied the "atomic" water to his daughter's warts and within a few short weeks the warts had completely disappeared. Many years later when Greig's daughter was in her thirties she came to him and asked if he had any of that atomic water left. Greig replied, laughing, "Oh, sweetie that was just regular tap water that I had put into that vial." Greig's daughter became upset because he had played such a trick on her. Looking back, Greig would have been better off to leave the hypnosis in effect and allow his daughter to continue believing in the atomic water.

Let there be no mistake, placebo and hypnosis are one and the same. Placebo is not something different or even a close cousin to hypnosis; placebo is an application of hypnosis. Placebo is waking hypnosis at its finest. If you see the word placebo used in relation to a study, you can just replace it with the word hypnosis; they are one and the same.

Even Pavlov found the placebo effect to be alive and well in dogs. Dogs that were given a few morphine injections for pain soon responded without even receiving the injection. In fact, just the technician coming into the room with the box containing the syringe would cause the necessary response.

Emile Coué also became aware of the placebo affect during his career as a pharmacist. Emile noticed that people would often respond positively to a remedy which should have not been affective. He also noted that when he gave high praise to the curative powers of some remedy the chances of the patient responding favorably increased amazingly.

For researchers and drug manufacturers, placebo is an annoyance. They will do anything to avoid the placebo. Yet testing a drug against a placebo is standard practice. Drug manufacturers would like their research and medications to stand alone and be effective by themselves, but no, there is that pesky placebo messing things up. It's particularly annoying when they work hard to develop a product and then the placebo actually out performs the product.

Medications are associated with all sorts of negative side effects such as weight gain, weight loss, depression, hair loss, suicide, loss of energy, hyperactivity, memory issues, trouble concentrating, loss of libido, heart attack, anal leakage, erectile dysfunction, death, and on and on. Do placebos have these negative side effects? Well, yes and no. Of course there is no negative side effects associated with a sugar pill or a sterile hypodermic. However during a placebo study, when people believe that they are getting the medication associated with that study, they will often develop some of the negative side effects (nocebo effect) even though they have only received a harmless placebo. If the mind believes that a certain outcome will occur, that is what tends to occur (refer to expectancy in the chapter on waking hypnosis).

Years ago I read *The Journals of Lewis and Clark*. Meriwether Lewis was not just an adventurer, he was also a physician. In Lewis's time becoming a physician meant that you created a relationship with a known physician and you followed him around learning the methods of medicine through the physician's mentorship.

During this era blood letting was the healing marvel of the day. As Lewis and Clark journeyed in search of a trade route to the west coast, they encountered many Indian tribes. Of course, there were plenty of Indians suffering from health issues, and Lewis worked to help cure their various maladies. There were many entries in the journal about the amazing successes Lewis experienced with the blood letting method.

Of course, we now know that blood letting wasn't curing anything. However the placebo effect was alive and well. Lewis also had a lot going for him in terms of hypnosis and especially waking hypnosis. Meriwether was a white medicine man and to these people, most of whom had never before seen a white man, his methods differed from those of their own medicine men. This imbued Lewis with special and magical powers in their minds. Blood letting wouldn't have been a huge leap for the Indians to accept compared to what they were already doing. And now here is this white medicine man from some far away land. He must possess powers and magic unheard of in this part of the world (which only amounts to more waking hypnosis).

Lewis and Clark made their way up the Missouri River in boats that were vastly different from the canoes the Indians used. The expedition had the latest in weaponry and they even had a cannon mounted to their boat, which was far more advanced than the bows and arrows the Indians were accustomed to. The white men could cause fire and explosions to occur, seemingly at will. To the Indians, seeing this expedition arriving would be no less astounding than us seeing a UFO landing in our own neighborhood now (a definite bypass of the critical factor). If a UFO did land in your neighborhood, wouldn't you expect them to possess some unknown powers?

The Indians, of course, were no strangers to the placebo effect; they had been making use of this power since ancient times. When the medicine man or woman did a healing, there would be all kinds of ceremony (waking hypnosis) to create the expectation that leads to the eventual cure. Of course, certain medicine men probably had more success than others due to the expectations that they created. A medicine man who was older might have been seen as wiser and more experienced, so he would have a better chance at succeeding with the same process than a younger person might.

Surely we are all aware of the country doctors who, when they didn't know what else to do with their patients, gave them a sugar pill and the patient was cured. That sugar pill is still being used, whether we are aware of it or not, and it is alive and well in medical studies where an actual sugar pill or some other benign substance is being used as the placebo. At one time what was referred to as a sterile syringe was used in the same way. The sterile syringe was nothing more than purified water injected as a cure which produced a beneficial physical response.

Let's say that after a new drug has been tested it is shown that the placebo was just as effective 35% of the time. That means that 35% of the people who were given or will be given that drug are also responding to the drug simply due to the placebo effect. The placebo effect, regardless of what researchers and drug companies may think, is a good thing, and if we really are going to help people, wouldn't it make sense to help them with something that is harmless to them rather than pumping chemicals into their bodies?

I was working with a client several years ago and she had recently moved to Colorado from the east coast. This woman was a substance abuse therapist. She told me that just prior to her moving to Colorado a man had come into her clinic who was a heroin addict and he wanted to get off of heroin.

She explained that part of the heroin addict's treatment was putting them on klonopin (chlonazepan) patches, an anti-anxiety medication. The patches provide a constant, steady dose. She told me that this client had been on the program two to three weeks before they realized that he was using the wrong part of the patch. He was taking the part of the patch with the medication in it and throwing it in the trash can and putting the sticky adhesive part on his arm, yet he was experiencing no withdrawals from heroine. As a hypnotist I *am* that sticky thing (placebo) for my clients.

My friend Grieg Thomson, whom I mentioned earlier, is a placebo and I mean that in the kindest possible way. In his 70s Grieg was the oldest graduate from our school. I often remarked that Grieg was a hypnotist before he ever walked in our door. What I mean by that is that Grieg was totally believable (waking hypnosis) in the role of hypnotist. He had the demeanor, the look, the authority, and the presence that created the perfect hypnotic effect. In a word Grieg was believable. If someone believes that the hypnotist has the power to help them then chances are good that that will occur.

If someone came into our office with an issue and I were to tell them that I was going to place them in the hands of one of our most seasoned veterans, and then turned them over to Grieg, they would experience positive results. "Seasoned veteran" could mean a lot of things and I am sure that Grieg is seasoned and a veteran of something. Some people might think that would be misleading, but isn't that what the placebo is doing? By letting you believe it is one thing, you gain the positive benefits of that thing as a result. Even though Grieg was very good at what he did, if I told someone, "I am going to turn you over to someone who just graduated a few weeks ago," it would create a different waking hypnosis (placebo effect) than if I present him in a more favorable light. It didn't matter that Grieg was a recent graduate, for he was still a seasoned hypnotist and he looked and filled the role perfectly. And that is hypnosis.

This is the waking hypnosis that I talk about in length in its own chapter. Any distinction between the placebo effect and waking hypnosis is a thin, blurry line. If we create the belief that a pill or a hypnotist has some special powers, then that is likely to be what occurs.

When a placebo study is being conducted those participants know that they are part of a placebo study; therefore they know there is a chance they are not getting the medication but some inert substance. What if those people were unaware that anyone in the study was receiving a placebo? How might that change the percentages? And what about the way the placebo is presented, and given, and by whom? The truth is different perceptions would change things a lot. In one study the recipients of a placebo did quite well; those who hadn't responded as well were given another placebo, only this time in the form of an injection, at which point those participants responded favorably. Apparently being given medication through a syringe is more powerful to us than in pill form. Another study showed that the color, size, and shape of a pill would cause a different response, even though it was an innocuous substance. Studies have shown that red, orange or yellow pills are associated with stimulants, while blue or green pills tend to make people drowsy. These are more examples of what I referred to as the nocebo response.

For the most part I would have to assume people doing placebo studies are not hypnotists and most placebo studies are directed at proving the effectiveness of the pharmaceuticals rather than the placebo. Even though the people conducting such studies may be attempting to stay unbiased, their unspoken (body language, attitude) waking hypnosis may be having an effect on the outcome. If the emphasis was creating more expectancy on the effectiveness of the placebo we would likely see the success of the placebo in these studies become even more apparent.

One might conclude that an individual must have to have a certain degree of gullibility for such nocebo responses to have an effect. Studies show that there does not appear to be any connection. Just because someone demonstrates a nocebo response in one study does not seem to make them more likely to respond similarly in another study. Even through testing and interviewing it is difficult to determine who might respond to a placebo or nocebo. However, true nocebo studies are not generally conducted due to ethical considerations.

There was a gentleman in the movie *My Big Fat Greek Wedding* who was running around everywhere with a dispenser of Windex. This bottle of Windex was his personal version of snake oil and he was using it for anything from healing cuts, to sunburns, to skin cancer, to fixing the Pontiac. His enthusiasm (waking hypnosis) created an expectation about the powers of Windex that even made these miracle cures believable to others around him.

Not unlike the Mr. Windex in the movie, those real snake oil salesmen of days gone by had waking hypnosis and the placebo effect working on their side. Before the days of modern medicine people were looking for any cure they could find to cope with health issues that were troubling them. If the snake oil salesman had a good shtick (hypnotic patter) he was creating powerful waking hypnosis and the customer's own desire to heal helped to create the placebo effect. If someone tried the snake oil and showed signs of improvement, then the placebo effect became even more likely (believable) for those who were witness to the cure. Is this wrong? Is the snake oil salesman who is getting positive results doing anything less ethical than some medical professional who is encouraging patients to take a pharmaceutical that is no more effective than the placebo, but has potentially life threatening side effects?

What about my friend Grieg, giving his daughter the make believe atomic water to cure her warts? Wasn't Grieg just another snake oil salesman misrepresenting his product? Or was Grieg being a more-intelligent-than-average, concerned parent who saved his daughter from the discomfort of a malady that may not have responded to some doctor recommended pharmaceuticals?

Don't get me wrong. There is a need for pharmaceuticals and I often send my clients for medications or to have their medications evaluated. But we have, perhaps, become too willing to accept whatever claims are made for a drug when there are other, more positive ways to accomplish the desired results. More doctors are becoming aware of this and are more open to alternative approaches. Lately doctors are becoming reluctant to prescribe antibiotics when they are not specifically indicated.

Nowadays drug companies go to a lot of trouble to make children's medications chewable, brightly colored, cherry and chocolate flavored, dinosaur shaped treats. When I was a kid many medications tasted horrible and I think that in our minds that may have made them more effective as well, or maybe somehow the vile tastes made us heal more quickly so that we wouldn't have to suffer through the abuse associated with the administration of another dose of castor oil or cod liver oil. Either way, hypnosis was having its positive effects upon us.

As long as we are on the topic of children, haven't most kids been helped by the placebo effect of that well known medicine woman and hypnotist, mom? What youngster didn't hear, "let mommy kiss it and make it better?" It works, too. Because mom creates the expectation that she can kiss a boo boo and make it go away, it does just that.

One of our graduate students, Dani Star, sent us this e-mail about a study using hypnosis for hot flashes in breast cancer survivors.

> Thursday, Sept. 25 (HealthDay-News) – Breast cancer survivors who suffer from hot flashes can reduce these attacks significantly with hypnosis, a new study finds.
>
> Hot flashes are a problem for many women who survive breast cancer. Not only do they cause discomfort, but they interrupt sleep, cause anxiety and affect a woman's quality of life.
>
> "This is a very encouraging study of hypnosis as a treatment for hot flashes in breast cancer survivors," said Dr. Ted Gansler, director of Medical Content at the American Cancer Society, who was not involved in the study. "This is an important topic because of the high prevalence of these symptoms in breast cancer survivors, and because few other treatment options are both safe and effective for this population," he added.
>
> There have been some other studies of hypnosis and cancer that indicate that the treatment is useful, but currently under utilized, Gansler noted.
>
> The report was published in the September issue of the *Journal of Clinical Oncology*.

For the study, researchers led by Gary Elkins, a professor of psychology at Baylor University School of Medicine, randomly assigned 60 breast cancer survivors who suffered from hot flashes to five weekly sessions of either hypnosis or no treatment.

During each session of hypnosis, women were given mental imagery and suggestions for relaxation and coolness. They were also told to disassociate themselves from hot flashes. In addition, they were taught to use positive suggestions and imagery during self-hypnosis.

Women who underwent hypnosis had an average 68 percent decrease in the frequency and severity of hot flashes, the researchers found. In addition, these women said they experienced less anxiety and depression. They also had significant improvements in sleep and their ability to perform daily activities, compared with women who received no treatment.

"Women are interested in alternatives to traditional hormone therapy and pharmacologic interventions, and this study demonstrates the feasibility and potential effectiveness of hypnosis as an alternative treatment," the researchers concluded.

But since the control group received no treatment, it's difficult to say whether some or even all of the improvement represents a "placebo effect," Gansler noted. "However, the researchers reasonably suggest that the improvement is so substantial that it is unlikely to be due entirely to a placebo effect," he said.

Nancy E. Avis, a professor in the department of social sciences and health policy at Wake Forest University School of Medicine, and author of an accompanying journal editorial, agreed that hot flashes are a symptom of cancer treatment that needs to be paid attention to.

"We don't have good interventions for hot flashes," Avis said. "We know that hormone therapy treats hot flashes, but women who have had breast cancer don't want to take hormone therapy," she said.

Many mind-body approaches are promising, Avis said. "The hypnosis study has impressive results, but we need more research," she said. "Based on these small studies, we are not ready to say they work."

Avis believes alternative approaches such as hypnosis are appealing to a lot of women. Many other approaches such as meditation and yoga are available at cancer centers, she noted.

"There is no reason to think they are not safe," Avis said. "The advice is—try it—there is no harm in trying. As long as you do it with somebody who knows what they are doing, there are no downsides," she said.

This type of research performed by universities and other researchers is quite valuable to the field of hypnosis and much more needs to occur. If this study had been done for a pill that gave a 68% decrease in the frequency and severity of hot flashes, doctors and sufferers would be all over it. When you consider the fact that there would be no negative side effects (unlike most pharmaceuticals) it becomes even more appealing.

I am a little concerned that even researchers at this level don't have a good understanding of hypnosis. Gansler noted that since there was no treatment given to the control group it is difficult to tell whether some or all of the improvement was due to the placebo effect. Give me placebo! I'll take all you have, give me bottles full of it, patches or injections, I don't care, give me more. It doesn't matter whether or not there was a placebo study, it's all hypnosis. Since there was no placebo study we would likely assume that there were no nocebo responses as well (not bad for 68%). It would have been interesting if the control group had been given something, for instance, a pharmaceutical or a placebo (injection, patch or pill), just for comparison.

It would make sense that if the control group had been given a placebo the results would have ended up around 68% as well, since both are really being given hypnosis. Any variations in the percentages between the hypnosis group and the placebo control group would represent the differences or effectiveness of different application methods of hypnosis or the differences in the groups themselves.

It is hard to know from this e-mail what was included in the study. Typically, anytime hypnosis is used in a study, very precise wording for suggestions or visualization are used. This is necessary so that there will be consistency and comparisons can be made. The problem is that whatever wording might be used may not be as effective as it could be. Also, it is likely that this type of research occurred in a group setting. This is fine; however, it is unlikely that the researchers were able to know each participant well. That is to say in individual sessions it is possible that the hypnotist would get to evaluate each person and vary wording and methods to better meet personal needs, thereby increasing the success rate even more.

Earlier in the study it said that participants were asked to disassociate themselves from the hot flashes. Giving an instruction like this can be problematic depending on how it is given. If that instruction was given in a conscious, waking state, it could make matters worse. If we consciously are trying to <u>not</u> think about or notice a particular symptom, it can serve to make that symptom more apparent than if we had not done anything. It is more effective if participants are given some strategy, such as associating pleasant feelings with the symptoms. If that type of dissociative method is given by saying, "Every time you feel these hot flashes, you will imagine yourself at the north pole" it can be effective, however it contains the statement that we will be having hot flashes, so we are creating an expectation that now hot flashes will occur and we can deal with them as they arise. What if we just used the hypnosis to end any hot flashes all together?

There was no explanation of the waking hypnosis leading up to the exercises in the study. I would think the waking hypnosis would be good, since researchers would be respected authority figures. From that point on it would be tough to speculate because we don't know what the expertise of the hypnotist(s) was or how well they understood waking hypnosis. It's not hard to imagine researchers as intellectual people. If they were to continue speaking and thinking and giving suggestions on an intellectual level there may have been poor waking hypnosis and suggestions.

Another problem with research and waking hypnosis is that research has an inherent problem. In order to determine how effective the hypnosis process has been the researchers have to do something that is very anti-hypnotic, and that is to follow up with the participants and determine how effective the methods have been. This is a necessary part of research, but it can be counterproductive. The very act of questioning participants creates an unwanted waking hypnosis. Let's say that some scale or scales were used to determine a participant's level of discomfort in connection with their hot flashes. At some point(s) after they have done hypnosis, the researchers need to follow up and determine the effectiveness of the treatment.

If the researchers say things such as, "where do you fall on this level of discomfort now?" or "how bad are the hot flashes now?" this questioning causes the participant to focus on the negative symptoms and therefore can cause them to recreate them. By bringing focus to the unwanted symptoms, we just recreate those symptoms (exactly what we don't want). By asking follow up questions we also create doubt in the participant's minds as to whether what we did was actually effective.

If this type of research were done differently we might be able to raise that 68% even further. What if by just being more careful about the waking hypnosis, or working with each participant individually, we could raise the effectiveness another 15%? Now we're up around 80% effectiveness. Pretty good for a "medication" that has no negative side effects associated with it!

There are so many variables that go into the study of hypnosis in research that it becomes difficult to nail down specific percentages that will occur consistently. A different person using the same verbiage could get a significantly different (better or worse) response. It could have to do with the presenter's credibility as a hypnotist or researcher, their confidence, or their skills as a hypnotist. The mood and type of audience, even the weather or the political atmosphere of the country could have an effect on the outcome. The Mayo Clinic has been using and studying the effectiveness of hypnosis for a long time and there is a statement on their website regarding their research on hypnosis and all of the variables.

"The physician's belief in the treatment and the patient's faith in the physician exert a mutually reinforcing effect; the result is a powerful remedy that is almost guaranteed to produce an improvement and sometimes a cure."

Petr Skrabanek and James McCormick,
Follies and Fallacies in Medicine, Page 13.

Just two days ago I had a client tell me his doctor had given him a placebo for a medical issue because he had not responded to other treatment. The doctor told him that he was being given a placebo and said that most people responded well to it. My client responded well to the placebo also, even though he was aware that he was taking an inert substance. He continues to take it to this day, enjoying the positive effects that he receives. Even though this might seem strange, I assume the doctor had heard that a certain percentage of people had responded to this placebo and so he just went with that, thinking it could have the same effects on someone else.

My client's physician wouldn't seem to be much of a hypnotist, yet even when he told his patient that he would be taking an inert substance that most people responded well to, that was enough hypnosis to cause a positive response. I expect this client will be a very good subject for me to work with.

In an article *The Placebo Effect* by Annemarie Colbin, PhD (2004) Annemarie talks about listening to a report on the radio that antidepressant drugs do not perform any better than a sugar pill, or placebo, in overcoming depression. Later that evening on the TV, the same news was mentioned and a man who had been through serious clinical depression joined the clinical trial of an antidepressant drug and got much better, later finding out he'd been on a placebo.

In an article by Christine Kaminski (2003) *The Placebo Effect: Redefining the Role of the Mind* Christine refers to another study of antidepressants where the placebo was effective 75% of the time—virtually the same as the active medication.

Christine goes on to quote another research of medications for asthma in which participants were given the same placebo twice, but, because they were told it was something different each time, they had totally different responses.

Christine went on to talk about how the brain actually responds differently depending on the need. "The mind therefore must have the ability to discern what is a placebo and what is an 'active' substance (or experimental drugs). The mind therefore must have the ability to discern what is a placebo and what is an experimental, and thereafter generates a physical response accordingly. This sophisticated ability of the mind to discriminate further shows us that the mind is a complex organ capable that is not fooled, but creates very informed responses."

I like what these women have to say on the subject. I think that the mind is not distinguishing between a placebo and an active substance, as Christine suggested. The hypnosis is more like this: Because the mind is given a suggestion to heal through the presentation of a pill or other treatment, the subconscious then proceeds in what ever manner is needed.

Our bodies are always pursuing optimal homeostasis (normal health). If we break a bone, catch a virus, or cut ourselves, the body works to achieve its homeostasis. The bones will begin to mend and grow back together. Blood will clot at the site of the cut, the bleeding stops, and cells begin to grow back together. The immune system works to fight off infections, etc. If we put a bandage on or apply antiseptics we could be using a placebo (encouraging the healing process) but we don't care. And we don't have to concern ourselves as to whether or not the mind is choosing a different strategy based on whether or not it has received a placebo or an active treatment. The subconscious knows how to heal itself, and it does it all the time, whether or not we take an active role.

I find it particularly interesting that antidepressants come up so frequently in these studies and how well placebos do in these tests. As a teenager I suffered for many years with severe depression. My family took no interest in anything that was less obvious than a broken leg and I went untreated. I finally got to a point in my life where I was unwilling to put up with it and became determined to move ahead. I did, and, as a result, I have been free of depression ever since. The only medication or treatment that I received was my own will to create a change. Because I gave myself the suggestion that I was going to create change, and that nothing else would be acceptable, I gained the positive healing that I desired.

I know that by simply changing our thoughts and through hypnosis (or other non-chemical methods) we can achieve freedom from depression, without the negative side effects.

One might want to consider the ethics of this as well. Is it ethical for a drug company to promote the use of a medication they know through research is not anymore effective than a benign substance or treatment, especially when that medication is shown to have negative side effects that can decrease libido, increase depression, cause weight gain, weight loss, suicide and more? I'm all in favor of making money, and lots of it, but are we in the business of profiteering on well being and making money no matter what the cost? Personally, I enjoy sleeping well at night.

Another thing to consider is the Active Placebo. These are placebos which are benign yet contain some side effects which might mimic the experimental medications. For instance an active placebo may give a participant dry mouth, which may be similar to side effects associated with the test medication. It is found that when this side effect occurs it causes a greater placebo response even though it is a benign substance.

For the most part the active placebo would seem like a good idea however, pharmaceutical manufacturers also manufacture placebos and active placebos. This gives them an opportunity to create and active placebo which may have side effects very similar to their pharmaceuticals. So far so good, but have you ever heard an advertisement for a pharmaceutical where there were headaches and other negative side effects which are similar to sugar pills or other placebo? Could it be that the active placebo they are giving to the placebo group is designed to give these side effects so that it looks like their product is no more dangerous than a sugar pill?

What about our diets—could that have a placebo effect? Certainly it would make sense that if our diet is lacking in some way (we could even be exhibiting symptoms of malnutrition), eating a more balanced diet would provide us with the vitamins and nutrients that our bodies are lacking and improved health and energy level would result.

What if we are eating a healthy diet (or think we are) and we experience an increase in vitality, even when our level of health couldn't be attributed to our diet? What if our enjoyment of good health and energy was simply a product of the placebo effect? We know that the average American does not eat an optimally healthy diet. Fat and cholesterol levels are way too high and we are experiencing an epidemic of type II diabetes.

I have been a vegetarian for many years and I enjoy healthy checkups and a cholesterol level way below the national average. Vegetarians statistically do much better in all areas of health and are much less likely to have weight issues. What if, more than anything, it was the <u>belief</u> that being vegetarian was playing a role in our enjoyment of good health? Isn't that putting the placebo response to good use?

"Forty years ago, a young Seattle cardiologist named Leonard Cobb conducted a unique trial of a procedure then commonly used for angina. Doctors made small incisions in the chest and tied knots in two arteries to try to increase blood flow to the heart. It was a popular technique—90 percent of patients reported that it helped—but when Cobb compared it with placebo surgery in which he made incisions but did not tie off the arteries, the sham operations proved just as successful. The procedure, known as internal mammary ligation, was soon abandoned."

The Placebo Prescription by Margaret Talbot,
New York Times Magazine, January 9, 2000.

It's good to see that this placebo (sham surgery) ended an apparently unnecessary surgery. How often is a surgery performed which could have been resolved with a placebo? I would guess that a sham surgery would have a greater placebo effect than a benign substance, simply because it is more involved.

I have wondered about the placebo effect and the different stop-smoking pharmaceuticals. In my opinion, any method that we use to stop smoking is hypnosis. Whether we stop on our own, use some pharmaceutical, or hypnosis itself, it's all hypnosis. It seems strange to me that using nicotine patches, gum or lozenges could help anyone get off of nicotine. Putting more nicotine into our systems would only seem to maintain the nicotine addiction. We could argue that it allows the individual to cut slowly down on the nicotine; however, cutting down has been shown to be one of the least effective ways of stopping smoking. If I gave nicotine patches or gum to someone who was not addicted to nicotine, wouldn't they become addicted to nicotine? If someone came to me to get off of heroine I wouldn't give them more heroine.

What about those people who were part of the placebo study for a nicotine replacement patch or pill and stopped smoking on the placebo? Nicotine is said to be more addictive than heroine or cocaine, yet here are people who stopped smoking with only the aid of an inactive substance. I would venture to say it is likely that they did better than those who went through the study getting nicotine added to their systems.

Doesn't it make sense that when someone puts a patch on their arm, they are giving themselves a hypnotic suggestion (creating expectancy, hypnosis) that what they are doing is going to cause them to be a non-smoker? The instructions say that you are to take this patch, and then that patch, and so on, until, in so many days you are a non-smoker (again creating mental expectancy, hypnosis). Any sort of pill or patch is going to create this mental expectancy (hypnosis) that will lead us to become a non-smoker. Plus, this so-called medication is prescribed by that famous waking hypnotist, your doctor.

Even the person who stops smoking on their own is making use of hypnosis. Their own desires and determination create their own hypnosis which is what causes the desired outcome to occur.

The placebo (hypnosis) is alive and well in our world and we need to embrace it and tap into the positive effects, rather than try to explain it away and thus ignore its value.

When we go to see an acupuncturist, naturopath, chiropractor, herbalist, psychologist, aroma therapist, hypnotist, shaman or allopathic MD aren't we, at least part of the time, responding to a placebo?

That benign substance, procedure, sham surgery, sterile syringe, sugar pill, etc. is only a placebo by limited definition. That sugar pill or placebo procedure is the application of hypnosis, and very powerful hypnosis, in the form of a waking suggestion.

Our subconscious wants us to heal (achieve homeostasis). We can aid this process by putting a cast on a broken limb, stitching and bandaging a wound, taking in fluids or removing some obstacle to achieving that homeostasis. But, for the most part, it is the subconscious mind that is doing the healing not some lab technician at Glasco, Smith, Klein.

Chapter 8

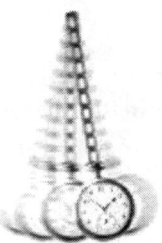

CONDITIONED RESPONSE

Here we are, back to the subject of Salter's book *What is Hypnosis* at the point where he focused on conditioned, or Pavlovian, response. While conditioned response definitely is hypnosis, it is just one piece of the hypnosis puzzle, much like the blind men describing the elephant from a limited experience of the animal.

This whole topic of conditioned response could easily be a book on its own, much as Salter wrote. While many in the field of psychology have made use of conditioned response, most of them probably are not aware that it is hypnosis. Salter even said that "psychotherapy is a matter of conditioning." Certainly, conditioned response is alive and well in behavioral therapy.

Pavlov never set out to discover conditioned response, just as the company 3M didn't originally set out to manufacture sandpaper or *Post-It* notes.

Pavlov was studying the digestive systems of dogs, and dog saliva, and its effects on food. He noticed that the dogs would begin to salivate prior to the appearance of food. What he found exploring what he referred to as "psychic secretion" and then "conditional reflex" was more exciting than dog saliva (imagine that). The fact that Pavlov stumbled onto conditioned response doesn't detract from the validity and importance of his contribution, for which he was awarded a Nobel Prize in 1904. Oftentimes, as occurred for Pavlov, 3M, and Christopher Columbus, when we are searching for one thing, an even more important discovery comes to the surface. It could be just the fact that we are searching that creates profound discovery.

We commonly associate Pavlov with ringing a bell during his dogs' feeding time, causing the association of the ringing bell and feeding to become engrained to the point where just ringing the bell caused the dogs to salivate. This was only one of many auditory and visual stimulus that Pavlov made use of. Some individuals have even expressed doubt that he ever actually used a bell.

There are many terms that refer to Pavlov's phenomenon: conditional response, conditioned response, Pavlovian response, conditioned reflex, associative reflex, classical conditioning, orienting response, Pavlovian conditioning, unconditioned stimulus, unconditioned response, conditioned stimulus, reflex response. I find no need to go into the intricacies of these terms for the purpose of this text, however there is an abundance of information about Pavlov and conditioned response available elsewhere.

Once the conditioned response is in effect (whether in dogs or humans), it takes no volitional thinking. A conditioned response is a purely subconscious response (habit, if you wish). Salter, in his book *What is Hypnosis* (ring a bell?), cited an experiment by C. V. Hudgins who, using methods similar to Pavlov, conditioned the pupil of a subject's eye to contract on command. First he conditioned the pupil using a light and ringing a bell.

The subject was then trained to use a hand grip in conjunction to ringing the bell and soon the operator was saying "relax" in conjunction with the bell and handgrip. The "relax" command was changed to "contract." Eventually all it took to contract the pupil was the operator's command "contract." It is amazing that we could, through a simple command, cause a normally involuntary response to occur.

Couldn't we consider the command "contract," when given by the operator, to be a posthypnotic suggestion? One could argue that it is not a posthypnotic suggestion because the man was not in a state of hypnosis at the time the association was made. However, we could easily argue that he was in a state of hypnosis whether or not a formal trance had been induced. It would be easy to imagine this subject sitting in a chair (perhaps a very comfortable chair) while light is being shone into his eye and bells are ringing and his hands are engaged in gripping. It could be easy to imagine that this must have occurred over some length of time to get to the point where the pupils were responding simply to the command "relax," and later to "contract." Certainly, it would be easy to imagine that within that time the subject may have become relaxed or bored or in some other way *informally* induced into a state of hypnosis. At the very least, and depending on what definition one might use, waking hypnosis was in effect; and if a suggestion is given in waking hypnosis, which is used again later to produce a particular result, then isn't that suggestion now a posthypnotic suggestion?

We used conditioned response long before Pavlov ever studied it. Canine response is one area in which we have been making use of this phenomenon for a long time. People have asked me if their dog can be hypnotized and my answer is, "sure and we already do (hypnotize them)." When Old Blue is lying around relaxing in the family room with everyone else and you're sitting there rubbing him behind the ears, you are creating a conditioned response. Old Blue now associates being rubbed behind the ears with feeling relaxed. When something else happens, like a stranger coming to the door, Old Blue begins to howl, and what do you do? Well, you rub Old Blue behind the ears and he begins to relax.

Not only have you made use of conditioned response, you weren't even aware of it. On top of that, Old Blue wasn't the only one who benefited from conditioned response because you were conditioned in the same way. Yes, when you were sitting there in the family room rubbing Old Blue behind the ears you weren't (likely) thinking, "Oh, I'm rubbing Old Blue behind the ears right now so that when someone comes to the door I can calm him down by rubbing him behind the ears." However, it did become engrained in your subconscious and you automatically (subconsciously) began rubbing him behind the ears to cause him to relax (imagine that).

This is what we refer to in hypnosis as anchors and triggers; conditioned response is nothing more than anchors and triggers (stimulus response). When one thing (feeling) is associated with another stimulus (anchor), it becomes engrained in our subconscious. For instance when you were rubbing Old Blue behind the ears that rubbing became associated (anchored) with the relaxed sensations that he was experiencing in the moment. Later, when someone came to the door and Old Blue got excited, rubbing Old Blue behind the ears, the stimulus associated with the relaxed sensations now becomes the "trigger" which causes the relaxed sensations to come to the surface.

Was Old Blue hypnotized when the association of being rubbed behind the ears and relaxation were created? I think we would have to answer yes to that. The relaxed state for Old Blue was hypnosis. Can we hypnotize animals? Yes, and while animals may not have much of an intellectual capacity to deviate from (or that I.Q. above 70 that we proclaim as necessary), they can be hypnotized, so isn't the rubbing behind Old Blue's ears now a post hypnotic suggestion? Check out *Animal Hypnosis* by Dr. F.A. Volgyesi 1963 Wilshire Book Co.

When my wife, Lynsi, and I get ready to take our dog, Scout, for a walk, Lynsi has a certain pair of heavy socks that she puts on first. Whenever Scout sees Lynsi put on those socks she gets all excited and ready to go for her walk. The socks were anchored with going on a walk and now when Lynsi puts them on (trigger) that is all it takes for Scout to get excited. Scout had that association created so strongly that once in the middle of the night Scout was not feeling well and needed to go outside. To communicate her needs to us she went and got Lynsi's socks and placed them by her on the bed.

When we are out walking and I need Scout to come back to me, I whistle and she comes. The reason that Scout knows to come is because as she came to me before, I whistled and so we created an anchor and trigger association. It wouldn't matter if I had used a bell to get that response or some other method; it is still a conditioned response. Conditioned response is not a new thing when it comes to training dogs, or in other areas.

Scout loves cheese and, no matter how quietly I open a cheese wrapper, she comes running from remote areas of the house to get her share. The sound of a cheese wrapper opening and the treat of getting cheese created an anchor and trigger (conditioned response) response within Scout. Lynsi and I were in Omaha not long ago and Scout was in Denver. When I opened a cheese wrapper in Omaha I commented to Lynsi, "I'll bet Scout's ears just perked up."

When I was around 11 years old, I was playing on a swing making myself spin around in circles. I continued this activity until I finally managed to make myself sick. The smell of Fritos was involved in the moment (anchoring Fritos to feeling sick) and from then on the smell of Fritos made me feel nauseous. I knew that there was nothing wrong with eating Fritos. Even as a young person I knew that it was the association I had created that day rather than something inherently wrong with Fritos. However, it took me many years before I could break that association and once again eat Fritos.

Did the smell of Fritos become a post hypnotic suggestion in itself? Was I hypnotized when that association was created? I would have to say yes once again. Being a young boy playing on the swing could easily mean I was in an imaginative (hypnotic) state. Spinning around on the swing until I made myself sick certainly created an altered state of consciousness (hypnosis). When the sick, dizzy feelings became associated with the smell of Fritos, that smell became my post hypnotic suggestion. Not unlike rubbing Old Blue behind the ears, or Scout's socks, whistle and cheese wrappers, Fritos became a post hypnotic suggestion.

Anchors and triggers (conditioned response) are a bigger part of our world than we probably realize. When we are in class and the school bell rings, our mood shifts dramatically to being full of excitement; either it's time to go out on the playground or to go home for the day.

Have you ever noticed when an old song comes on the radio how quickly that song can bring back feelings and memories that were associated with that song from long ago? Those feelings could be from one end of the spectrum to the other, but because that song was playing at the time you were experiencing certain feelings, the two things have become associated (anchored) in your subconscious. Now, when that song plays again (trigger) the association between those two things comes right back to the surface. On a rainy day, some people may feel blue; others, like Gene Kelly, dance in the rain. It just depends on how we became conditioned to the rain.

To clarify these responses without belaboring the point I will give you this distinction about the responses. Scout exhibited a normal unconditioned response when she came running back to Lynsi and me while we were out walking. There is safety, comfort, even joy (if you will) for returning to her pack (us) and therefore a benefit (stimulus). This is a normal response for a dog or any sort of pack animal. When I added a whistle to her returning to us, I then created the conditioned (Pavlovian, learned) response. Now, anytime I whistle, because it has become associated with returning to her pack, she returns. That whistle, when it was first associated with returning to the pack, created a conditioned stimulus (an anchor). Later, when I use it to call her back to us, it triggered the feelings associated with the comfort of being with the pack.

When I was a youngster, a friend of mine had a little dog with an injured paw. The dog had to be taken to the veterinarian's office to have her paw stitched and bandaged. Of course, the paw gave the little dog some discomfort and she would hold her paw up and whine quite frequently. When she would hold her paw up and whine, some loving family member would hold her and give her attention. Years after the little dog's paw had healed she would hold it up and whine anytime she wanted attention.

The little dog had learned (conditioned response) that holding her paw up would get her love and attention anytime she wanted it, and for her, it no longer had anything to do with the injury.

Of course, no *human* has ever learned that feigning a headache or backache or some other health ailment could serve them in some way. Having a headache might get us a back or neck rub from a caring spouse, or get us out of that test or band concert that we were dreading.

When Pavlov first noticed that the dogs were salivating it could have been due to smells or sounds, although it was actually first due to people wearing lab coats (unconditioned stimulus or trigger) which the dogs associated with mealtime. This was the unconditioned response which he first believed was a psychic secretion. Later when the smells or sounds of food being prepared occurred, or people in lab coats appeared, Pavlov would ring a bell or use some other conditioned (learned) stimulus to be associated (anchored) with food. Later on, just the ringing of the bell (trigger) would cause the dogs to salivate.

If the only time someone takes the dog in the car is when the dog needs to go to the veterinarian that dog is likely to create an uncomfortable association with riding in the car. Riding in the car has become anchored to the discomfort of going to the vet, so any time the dog is encouraged to get in the car (trigger), the dog will likely resist or become nervous.

If, instead, we use the car to take the dog to the lake or the dog park, then riding in the car will be anchored to good feelings and the dog will be willing to go along, even if we do end up at the vet's.

Another place where anchors and triggers come into play (an area that everyone should be aware of) is when we go to sleep at night. Normally sliding into the sheets at night has become anchored to falling directly off to sleep. So whenever we do slide under the sheets at night a natural trigger response (expectation) occurs that we will drift right off to sleep.

Two things and two things only should occur when we go to bed at night. Those two things are sleeping and making love. And both of those should lead to a good night's sleep.

Some people have lost their normal trigger to fall asleep at night. When people use the bed for things other than the two things that I mentioned, they may find themselves having difficulty falling asleep at night. Often people will use the bed to perform all sorts of things that are not falling asleep. For instance, people will lie in bed for hours paying the bills, talking on the phone, working on the computer, watching TV, or performing other duties that have nothing to do with sleep. The result is that the bed has become associated with things that have nothing to do with sleeping or having sex and the trigger to fall asleep when we slide in under the covers is now gone.

If you are someone who has been having trouble falling asleep, you may recognize what I am talking about. By simply removing the TV and other distractions from the bedroom and limiting the bed to just the two activities that I mentioned, we can once again create the anchor and trigger response that is so desirable. If you do not find yourself falling asleep right away, there is no reason to lie in bed thinking about it. Get up and go do the dishes or vacuum or some other fairly mindless yet productive activity, and then return to bed until the desired sleep does occur. Lying in bed thinking about how you are not falling asleep and, of course, there <u>is</u> that important meeting tomorrow that you want to be alert for, will not help to create the anchor and trigger response that is needed. That is why it is advisable to get up and remove yourself from the bed until that anchor and trigger becomes successfully created. Then, each time you crawl into bed the expectation that sleep will occur takes over.

Once conditioned or unconditioned response (anchors and triggers) becomes engrained in the subconscious no volition is required to maintain it (habit). This can be a good thing, or not, depending on what it is that has been engrained in the subconscious. The nice thing is that through hypnosis we can use this type of response to create more positive behaviors in our world with relative ease.

For more on anchors and triggers check my book *The Power of the Past*.

So, from a hypnotist's point of view conditioned response comes down to a matter of anchors and triggers and post hypnotic suggestion.

Chapter 9

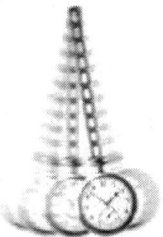

CONCLUSION

I hope that you have enjoyed this hypnotic journey, and I hope that, if nothing else, I have stimulated some thought and caused you to think about hypnosis somewhat differently. Hypnosis has been an amazing journey and occupation, and the longer I am involved in this field the more excited I become. The subconscious is a huge world to explore and we may have only scratched the surface as far as tapping into this amazing resource.

So what is hypnosis?

I wish I could just give you a single, succinct sentence defining hypnosis, but that would be much like encapsulating the meaning of life in a few words.

When Leslie Le Cron attempted to define hypnosis in his book *The Complete Guide to Hypnosis* he just said, "That was a very difficult question to answer." He went on to say, "We can describe it, but no one has yet come up with a theory which will fit in every aspect."

I like what Masud Ansari, PhD had to say, as I quoted in the beginning of this book, which was basically *it's very hard to describe this elephant.* As a result, it is easy to understand why so many experts in this field have not been able to come up with a nice, neat definition of hypnosis that is correct and works in all situations.

I included another definition in the first chapter of this book to show where hypnosis has been and how people have thought of it in the past. That definition is the one by WM. Wesley Cook AM, MD. Dr. Cook was Professor of Physiological Medicine in the National University of Chicago at the time.

To reiterate, his definition was as follows:

"Hypnotism is the science and art of mentally controlling the thoughts and actions of others. Its study embraces a knowledge of the methods best adapted for developing personal mental power and directing the mental activity of others."

This definition flies in the face of what we know hypnotism to be. But it does demonstrate how hypnotism was viewed by some in the past (some still view it this way). Fortunately, the belief that the hypnotist ("operator") possessed power over his/her client or that the client was under the hypnotist's control is mostly a thing of the past. Yet it is not hard to see how fears about hypnosis have come to be when a supposed expert in the field defines hypnosis as controlling the subject's mind in a way that the operator desires. Not many people are likely to go running to their local hypnotist if they think someone will be taking control of their mind.

The copy of Dr. Cook's book *Practical Lessons in Hypnotism* that I have was reprinted in 1943, and there is no indication as to the original copyright date, so it may be very old. While there is some interesting and worthwhile information in Dr. Cook's book we can also observe how time and knowledge have changed our opinions about hypnotism.

When you think about it, modern hypnosis has been around for more than two hundred years; hypnosis is as old as mankind, and we are still trying to define it. That notion is even more mind boggling within the context of this book. Hypnosis is more common in our world than any other mental state, but we are still trying to recognize and understand it.

It may be part of our human nature to try to compartmentalize something so as to understand it better. Perhaps there is no compartment big enough for this particular elephant and personally I'm fine with that however, the general public would probably like a more definitive way to compartmentalize hypnosis that would alleviate their fears.

One thing I am very sure of is that hypnosis is a state of the organism (don't you love being referred to as an organism?). Describing hypnosis—as some of the definitions do—as a state of suggestibility, or heightened suggestibility, or self-regulating, or softening of psychic defenses, or operating theory, or heightened awareness, or desire to follow the instructions of the hypnotist are not definitions of hypnosis at all, but descriptions of conditions of hypnosis. That is to say, hypnosis is a state. The so-called definitions are just characteristics of that state.

Of all of the short definitions of hypnosis that I gave in the beginning of this book the one that I like and have used most is the one from Jerry Kein: "Hypnosis is the bypass of the critical factor of the subconscious mind and the establishment of selective thinking." Even so, this description is also very limiting.

I was interviewed on a local radio show the other day by my good friend and fellow hypnotist, Lee Rindner. One of the first things out of Lee's mouth was the question of how do *I* define hypnosis? I laughed and told him I was right in the middle of writing this book in order to answer that very question. We chatted a bit and then Lee said, "I just say that <u>any</u> subconscious response is hypnosis." I'm not sure if Lee realizes just how profound that simple statement is, but if you have been following along with this book, you know that almost everything I have expressed has to do with subconscious response.

We go around in the world focusing on the conscious mind. Thinking, concentrating, memorizing, studying for that PhD, and on and on. Our world seems to center upon—and to reward—that conscious, analytical thinking though it makes up only the smallest part of the equation. Yes, we do need that conscious, intellectual mind, and it does serve us, but the subconscious is really what it's all about.

Thomas Edison had a little cubby hole that he used to sneak off to during the day to take what he referred to as little catnaps. During these little catnaps (hypnosis) he came up with all sorts of ideas for inventions. Edison knew the secret for not only tapping into his own subconscious mind but putting it to work for him. Try it, you'll like it.

So now my new favorite one line definition of hypnosis is that of Lee Rindner's:

"Any subconscious response is hypnosis."

So! What would that make hypnotherapy? My answer to that is:

"Any positive, subconscious change which occurs in an individual that is aided by the guidance of a hypnotherapist or through self-hypnosis is hypnotherapy."

If you like the broad definition of *Altered States of Consciousness* that I used earlier then another definition to try on for size is:

"Any altered state of consciousness is hypnosis."

Glossary of Hypnosis Terms

I have often thought that a good glossary of hypnosis terms would be very useful. I have tried to keep this glossary fairly main-stream and I am sure that I have not included enough for some individuals, however I hope that most readers will find this useful.

Abreaction: An emotional or physical response to an emotional stimulus. Can be a normal product of certain hypnotic processes or can be triggered during trance for any number of reasons.

Accessing Questions: Questions that encourage an experiential response within the client.

Act as if: See rehearsal technique.

Action Plans: See homework assignment.

Addiction: Addiction is commonly associated with chemical addiction to narcotics such as nicotine, cocaine, heroine, etc. We can also become addicted to other things such as other people, institutions, exercise, etc. Some addictions might be referred to as positive addictions such as exercise. Even exercise has chemical addiction associated with it in the form of neurotransmitters. An addiction typically has habitual activity connected with it but it is more than just pure habit. While changing a habit might cause us some stress, there are no real withdrawal symptoms associated with habit change. Addiction, on the other hand, has serious withdrawal symptoms associated with it.

Advertising: Hypnosis, whether or not the advertisers are always aware of it, is alive and well in advertising. Refer to advertising in the chapter *What Else is Hypnosis* and *The Fear of Hypnosis* for more on this topic.

Affect Bridge: Also somatic affect bridge. The emotions used in a hypnotic regression that allow the therapist to take someone back to the Initial Sensitizing Event (ISE). (Refer to *The Power of the Past* by this author).

Affirmations: Positive statements that are given to oneself or by someone else such as a hypnotist, to help create desirable changes. Affirmations are statements that are present tense, believable, achievable and measurable. The use of affirmations was popularized be Emile Coué. "Every day in every way I am getting better and better." Affirmations are a form of positive suggestion.

Afformations: Similar to affirmations, afformations make use of why. Examples, Why am I so lucky? Why am I so wealthy? Why am I so healthy? Unlike affirmations when we ask why we are declaring that the positive thing we desire is in our possession and now the mind is on an expedition to prove it rather than to break down old paradigms on why we don't have these things. Why do you enjoy afformations so much?

Age progression: A sort of opposite to age regression. By moving the client ahead into the future we can determine where our current actions will lead us (a sort of crossroads) to encourage positive change, or it can be to further anchor the positive success we have had in trance and to cause them to move ahead into the future. It also is a way to put to test what we have done in trance and becomes a convincer for the client. If the client does not find themselves in the future with the new positive changes there may be more work to do.

Agreement: For formal hypnosis to occur, whether for clinical or entertainment purposes, a willingness (consent) whether stated or implied by the subject must be present.

Agreement Principle: The subconscious mind follows what it is instructed to do. See Compliance Principle.

Aha experience or Aha psychology: That moment of realization when (the light comes on) a shift happens. In hypnosis, this is often what happens in a regression at the moment of reaching the ISE or through a Gestalt. This is what a lot of hypnotists have relied on in the past to make that shift in behavior at the ISE.

Alpha: The first level entering deeper consciousness.

- 7-14 CPS (cycles per second of brainwave activity)
- The beginning of inner consciousness levels
- Self hypnosis
- Meditation
- E.S.P.
- Increased suggestibility
- Time distortion
- Sleep, including R.E.M. sleep, begins

Alpha is said to be the level at which we have equal access to the conscious and subconscious mind.

Altered States of Consciousness: Any state of consciousness that deviates from our normal state of consciousness and can mean a wide range of experience. Altered states can be normal and natural or induced through the use of some substance. Some people are fearful of the term altered states of consciousness, however, for the most part these states are very natural. Hypnosis is an altered state of consciousness.

AMA: The American Medical Association sanctioned the official use of hypnosis in 1958.

Ambiguous suggestions: Suggestions that are not straightforward in their meaning, and could have more than one meaning, which allows the subconscious to take whatever meaning from the suggestion that works for it.

Amnesia: Loss of memory. Can be caused by an emotional or physical trauma and may be selective to certain time periods. A client's ability to create amnesia during hypnosis is an indication of depth of trance.

Amnesia for the hypnotic experience can sometimes be a result of the client's expectations or produced by suggestion on the part of the hypnotist.

Analgesia: A reduction in sensation. Analgesia could be the goal in hypnosis or a step toward getting total anesthesia.

Anesthesia: total numbness, lack of feeling in any given area of the body.

Anesthetic Hypnosis: Even under chemical anesthesia and during surgery the subconscious mind is open to suggestion. It is advised that doctors and others in the operating room be aware of what they say so as not to create a negative effect on the patient.

Anchors: When one thing becomes strongly associated with another an anchor has been formed. Climbing into bed and sleeping are two things that are anchored together. The smell of popcorn and the movies are two things that are anchored with one another. For some, getting behind the wheel of their car and lighting a cigarette are things that have become anchored together. See triggers.

Animal Magnetism: A term made popular by Franz Anton Mesmer who, among others of his day, employed magnets to achieve the healing state that was called Mesmerism and is now hypnosis.

Mesmer asserted that while observation reveals how the planets mutually affect one another in their orbits, and the moon controls the earth's ocean tides, these spheres also exert a direct action on all parts that make up animate bodies, particularly the nervous systems of such, by an all-penetrating fluid. This action manifests itself through intensification and the remission (expansion and contraction) in the body.

He maintained that just as the sea manifests ebb and flow, so the force in the body will expand and contract. He called this property of the animal body that renders it liable to the action of the heavenly bodies and of the earth, *animal magnetism*. He suggested that while the stars might (have an) influence the human bodies themselves might carry a magnetic, curative fluid so that they could possibly have a healing effect on each other.

Anorexia Nervosa: An eating disorder (a kind of starvation) that is characterized by a distorted body image. This is a very complex issue and hypnotherapy can be a very useful tool, however the skilled hypnotherapist needs to be working directly with the client's health professionals because anorexia is a life threatening issue. Even though the client might not seem severely ill, certain behaviors common to anorexia put them at risk for sudden heart failure and other issues. There are copious amounts of information available and it is advised that all hypnotists familiarize themselves with the nature of this disorder so that, at the very least, the therapist can make an intelligent referral.

APA: The American Psychiatric Association approved the use of hypnotherapy in 1958.

Apex problem: Even though a change is obvious and observable by others the subject does not notice that a change has occurred. This phenomenon is common to hypnosis and TFT (Thought Field Therapy). When a change (habit) occurs quickly and easily it feels as if it is normal (has always been the case) and a sort of denial that it was ever any other way occurs. This is how it should be when hypnosis is successful because when the transfer of information (electrical energy) occurs it is as if that unwanted behavior never existed. At this point the client should walk out the door without ever having to give the problem another thought. Often the hypnosis or the therapist is not given any credit for the transformation (which some people may find disturbing). However, the main focus should be that the clients achieve their goals regardless of whether or not the therapist or the therapy gets recognition.

Aphasia: An unwillingness to talk, common in deeper states of hypnosis.

Apposition of opposites: suggestions that create simultaneous polarities of experience.

Arm Levitation: A form of catalepsy. Can be a test for trance depth level or for entertainment purposes.

Arons Depth Scale: A depth scale developed by Harry Arons and embraced by the National Guild that identifies six stages of hypnosis.

Artificial somnambulism: Has the appearance of somnambulism, but true amnesia has not occurred and therefore complete anesthesia is unlikely. This is also a term that was used by Puysegar to describe a mesmeric state that did not include convulsion (as was common with Mesmer) or unpleasant effects; the subject was able to open their eyes and talk in a slurred manner. Without being there to observe, it sounds like Puysegar was achieving a true somnambulism.

Assertive: Authoritarian, directive, commanding, paternal style. Used more extensively in regression work.

Authoritarian: A direct and commanding style. Stage hypnotists use an authoritarian style and it is also used in therapeutic sessions. It was the more common style with early hypnotists. See also Dominance-Submission relationship.

Auto Hypnosis: A term for self-hypnosis.

Autonomic nervous system: Physical functions that are taken care of more or less automatically, like our heart rate, blood pressure and breathing. While we can have a conscious effect on these things we normally don't give them much attention.

Auto suggestion: Auto suggestions are suggestions given to oneself. They may be given in a conscious or hypnotic state. When Emile Coué coined the term many years ago his intention was that they be used in a normal state of consciousness and with a lot of repetition.

Aversion: In hypnosis creating repugnance toward an unwanted behavior is aversion. For instance, creating an association with chocolate that causes it to have the qualities of feces is an aversion method.

Aversion therapy: Is a common form of therapy used in psychology that is used to eliminate unwanted behaviors through association of averse stimulus with an unwanted behavior. Showing smokers the diseased lungs of deceased smokers or showing them pictures of people smoking through tracheotomy tubes is a common form of aversion therapy. It is the effect on the subconscious mind (hypnosis) that makes these methods at all successful.

Awaken: See emerge.

BCH: Credentials for board certified hypnotist (hypnotherapist). These credentials are advanced credentials from the National Guild of Hypnotists. The person who has achieved BCH has had to have been in the practice of hypnosis for a specific amount of time, has had to have had continuing education, and is required to pass written and oral exams administered by members of the NGH board. Some hypnotists may refer to themselves as board certified, but if they have not met these requirements, they are not.

Behavioral Changes: Changes that are made in the client's normal, daily life. Shifting work habits, exercise, eating, or dealing with family and relationships in a better way are a few examples of behavioral changes.

Believability: How believable (credible) we are as a hypnotist and how easy it is to create expectancy helps to create the waking hypnosis and the positive outcome that we desire. See also expectancy and waking hypnosis.

Beta: This is the level of consciousness that we refer to as normal, waking consciousness.

- 14 to 21 CPS (cycles per second of brainwave activity)
- Considered to be normal, waking consciousness or outer world conscious level
- Normal physical action is experienced
- Normal physical world of sight, sound, touch, smell, and taste

Between life regression: It is believed by many that information is available to us between incarnations. It is believed that we meet up with past loved ones, friends, relatives, angels or spirit guides, and also that our own awareness may be clearer which gives us information that we can bring forth into our current existence. See also Life purpose regression.

Binaural Sounds (binaural beats): By listening (normally with headphones) to two slightly different frequencies from one ear to the other the mind tends to function in the frequency that is between those two frequencies. This can be a quick, easy method to cause someone to get into and stay (for a period) in certain brain frequencies that will cause certain positive results such as relaxation, meditation, creativity, learning, etc. Computerized machines are now available with a wide variety of options as far as programs and frequencies that one can make use of.

Bind of comparable alternatives: Ericksonian—a forced choice situation is created for the client where either choice will lead to the positive outcome that is desired. Example: will you enjoy leaving here a non-smoker at 3:00 or at half past the hour?

Biofeedback: Biofeedback machines are machines that give feedback (through sound or lights) to the individual indicating what brain frequencies they might be generating. By using different thought processes (visualization) a client can learn to produce brainwaves that are more consistent with the changes they desire, such as lower stress or anxiety.

Birth by Hypnosis™: Hypnosis for childbirth utilizing the deepest states of hypnosis. Developed by Lynsi Eastburn and Arthur Leidecker—of the non-profit HypnoFertility Foundation—as a natural progression of HypnoFertility˚ and Fertility by Hypnosis™. A success oriented standalone program, Birth by Hypnosis™ also serves as an advanced training for all childbirth educators.

BMA: British Medical Association approved the use of hypnosis in 1955.

Body Manipulation: By manipulating parts of the subject's body a trance state can be induced or deepened. Anchoring, acceptance of suggestions or movement in trance can also be encouraged through body manipulation.

Body sway test: a pre-hypnosis exercise (suggestibility test). Can be done as a rearward or forward test and is more advanced than a simple catalepsy or Chevreul's pendulum.

Boredom: A form of hypnosis. Boredom is also a method of induction. Many inductions use boredom at least in part (progressive relaxation, counting down the stairs, etc.) to take a client into trance.

Braid fascination technique: See hypnodisc.

Brain washing: Any effort aimed at instilling certain attitudes and beliefs in a person.

Bruxism: Teeth grinding, usually while asleep (impulse control disorder), can result in serious damage to the teeth. Hypnosis can be very effective for Bruxism.

Bulimia Nervosa: An eating disorder characterized by binges of eating large amounts of food (usually food of a high calorie or fat content) in a distinct amount of time. Purging (vomiting) following binges is common. As with anorexia nervosa, hypnotherapy can be helpful, however, also as with anorexia, the therapist needs to be qualified and in contact with (and referred by) the client's physician since bulimia can be life threatening as well (see anorexia nervosa). A new category is coming into existence that will cover binging only (without purging).

Calendar Method: A method of regression where the client and therapist regress by flipping back through a calendar. Can be done using ideomotor signaling and is also done with the therapist leading the client.

Candle Method: A method of using a candle to produce trance that was popular in the past. This method included holding a candle at a height that would cause eyestrain, hand passes, and suggestions of becoming tired or drowsy.

Catalepsy: Rigidity or tightening of various body parts. In hypnosis the phenomenon of catalepsy occurs in a way not common in a conscious state. We can create catalepsy in various parts of the body. Eye, arm and full body catalepsy are the most common. Catalepsy is a useful tool to help determine someone's level of trance and it also acts as a convincer and a crowd pleaser for entertainment purposes.

Catalyst Method: Other devices used to employ a trance state (Dave Elman). Elman liked to use his cigarette smoking method. Taking three puffs of the cigarette, each puff would take the client deeper and achieve eye closure. Taking a drink from a glass of water or tapping on the head was used similarly; virtually anything might be employed to achieve eye closure and hypnosis.

Catharsis: An extreme emotional response (purifying and relieving) common in some therapeutic work.

Catharting: The outward demonstration of catharsis such as crying, screaming and bodily contortions.

Catholic Church: Approved the use of hypnosis in 1957.

CCH: Credentials for certified clinical hypnotherapist as used by some accrediting bodies.

Cell Command: A type of hypnotherapy that relies on ideomotor signaling and a series of yes or no questions regarding a subject's particular issue. There are variations on this type of work, but it appears to be based on the work of Ed Martin.

Ceremony: Ceremonies are useful to create a certain hypnotic experience in hypnosis. They can be part of a process that helps to create a trance experience. See the chapter *What Else is Hypnosis* for more on ceremony and ritual.

CH: Credentials used by NGH members. Stands for certified hypnotist or certified hypnotherapist and now consulting hypnotist. The meaning can change depending on the individual's desires and the regulation of such terminology which can vary widely from state to state.

Chaining: A type of utilization method that places any thing that may be a perceived distraction into a suggestion that helps to nullify it. For instance: "Isn't it nice that the sounds of the road crew working outside provide you with the freedom to go deeper into hypnosis?" See also pacing and leading and sounds patter.

Changing Personal History: Ericksonian terminology for age regression.

Chemical Hypnosis: Hypnotic effects achieved through the application of chemicals. Sodium amytal, sodium pentothal and others have been commonly used in the past for this purpose.

Chevreul's Pendulum: A method often used as a suggestibility test or convincer. A person can achieve answers from their own subconscious through proper use of the pendulum. It can also be used for trance induction much like the pocket watch method. Early on it was used somewhat like an Ouija board with letters; the pendulum would move toward letters spelling out words or phrases. Now we tend to use it for more basic yes or no type questions.

CHt: Credential for certified hypnotherapist used by some organizations.

Clinical Hypnosis (Clinical Hypnotherapist): I am basing this definition loosely on a description that came to me from the NGH via Rev. Dr. C. Scot Giles. The entire description would be too lengthy to include here, but you may find it on the NGH website (www.ngh.net) or on the Eastburn website (www.hypnodenver.com).

There is no dictionary definition to which we can point to with authority. Much of the definition is ambiguous and those who do or do not use this term tend to have arguments for why they should or shouldn't. We could argue that all hypnosis that is aimed at helping people with their issues is clinical hypnosis. The term does tend to conjure up images of men and women with extensive degrees working in lab coats performing scientific studies or medical procedures in a controlled environment. This could be the case or it could also be that the person who is calling themselves a Certified Clinical Hypnotherapist has recently taken some correspondence course and has yet to see their first client.

I have encountered a number of people in the hypnosis field who do or would like to refer to themselves as a clinical hypnotherapist more out of ego than anything and the term may only vaguely refer to what they do. I have a credential on my wall that says I am a certified clinical hypnotherapist; however I never refer to myself in that way. I feel that who I am and what I do speaks for itself.

Coma State (also Hypnotic Coma): This is a term used by some hypnotists to describe the Esdaile State. This is not a term that should be used with the general public for it could cause unwarranted concern. This state is by no means a true coma and there is no way that anyone in this state could get stuck in hypnosis (which is an unfounded belief held by some).

Complementary: Serving as a complement; completing–mutually providing each other's needs. Hypnosis is complementary to other medical or psychological procedures.

Compliance Principle: The subconscious mind always moves in the direction that the conscious mind points it.

Compounding Anesthesia: If an amount of hypnotic anesthesia occurs then that can be strengthened to cause greater anesthesia.

Compounding (also compounding effect): Repetition causes suggestions to become stronger. See the rule of three.

Conditioned Reflex: See conditioned response.

Conditioned Response: Repeated exposure to a stimulus that is associated with a behavior will reactivate that behavior. This is a form of hypnosis. Also Pavlovian response. See also anchors and triggers.

Confusional suggestions: Confusion can be very effective in hypnosis whether it is part of the hypnotic patter that the hypnotist is using or through a specific suggestion. Confusion tends to dissociate the conscious mind and make the subconscious more available.

Confusion: Inductions, suggestions, stories, and patter that are confusing tend to overload the conscious mind and make the subconscious more available to the therapist.

Conscious: For our purposes the conscious mind is that part of the mind where intellectual, judgmental, critical, analytical thinking occurs as well as short term memory.

Consent: See agreement.

Contact: A method of induction whereby the hands were placed in various places and pressure applied. Mesmer used both hand passes and contact. Just placing a hand on someone's shoulder can cause a relaxing sensation. If we use gentle pressure with each exhalation and release on the inhale we create a pacing situation and a non-verbal induction. Contact methods have been used to hypnotize animals.

Content suggestions: Suggestions that are very descriptive of thoughts, feelings, emotions or other details. "Find yourself at the pond in the peaceful meadow. The yellow daffodils create a dreamy picture, the gentle breeze brings the scent of fresh sweet country air to your nostrils."

Converted Effort (the law of Converted Effort): will is not only powerless against suggestion, but only serves to strengthen the suggestion it seeks to destroy (Charles Boudouin). Basically this is saying that by trying to focus (will) our way away from what we don't want we only serve to create what we don't want. If someone wants to be a non-smoker and they put down their cigarettes and keep telling themselves *I don't want a cigarette, I'm not going to smoke, I'm not going to have a cigarette*, over and over that person's will is likely to lose the battle and the desire for yet another cigarette will win out.

Conversational Postulates: are an indirect way of giving a suggestion. Conversational Postulates are questions that can be answered with a yes or no answer, but are actually achieving another response. "Would you like to sit down and relax?" While the answer to this question could be yes or no the intended response is that the individual will sit down and relax.

Control: The subject in a hypnosis session is always in control; however willingness on the part of the client to suspend that control can be very productive in a hypnosis session. It is considered useful for the hypnotist to assume control during the hypnosis session.

Convincers: Simple tasks that the client is given in trance that help to convince the mind that something different is occurring and therefore that the hypnosis is working (see double bind).

Couéism: a term given to the methods of practice (autosuggestion, self suggestion) developed by Emile Coué. Couéism is built on two fundamentals: All suggestion is autosuggestion which is the action of "imagination" or of the "Mental." And will is overcome by imagination.

Counter suggestion: A suggestion that overrides the original suggestion. Sometimes these suggestions are given unintentionally and by some well-meaning but counterproductive Samaritan. A suggestion that chocolate tastes like rabbit droppings given to a client may be working well until some well-meaning friend says, "Eat some chocolate, you don't know what rabbit droppings taste like, they taste like chocolate." Now the original suggestion has been overridden.

Counter Transference: Occurs when the therapist projects his or her own emotional needs onto the client. Often this has to do with a sexual projection. Counter transference is not a good thing. The client's needs are what are to be met in a therapeutic session, not the therapist's.

Covering all possibilities: Suggestions where all possible responses lead to a positive outcome

Critical Faculty: According to Dave Elman, "The critical faculty is that part of the mind which passes judgment. It distinguishes between the concepts of hot and cold, sweet and sour, large and small, dark and light."

The critical faculty is made up of information (history) that we accumulate, particularly when very young, that forms a barrier to information that is different (whether or not that information is accurate). We operate in paradigms that are based on our critical faculty.

Critical Incident Process: Another term for age regression.

Crossroads: A technique that is good for decision making; a leverage technique. By bringing a client to a fork in the road we can paint a picture of what the outcome will be if they continue as they have been (smoking, for instance). Then we have them turn and look down the other, more positive road, without this unwanted behavior or other positive change in their life what happens in the future. This is a leverage technique and the mind tends to choose the more appealing option. For the best effect keep the undesirable scene on the left road and positive outcome on the right road.

Davis-Husband Scale: A popular depth scale that uses five major divisions to identify trance depth.

Deepening: A variety of methods used to assist someone into a deeper trance state. Using the Elman arm drop or focusing on the breathing are two common ways to deepen a client.

Dehypnosis (also dehypnotizing): As much as we might refer to ourselves as hypnotists or hypnotherapists, a lot of the work that we do is really dehypnotizing people from the unwanted hypnosis they have received in the past.

Dehypnotize: See dehypnosis. Dehypnotize is also a term sometimes used for emerging from hypnosis.

Delta: Delta is an extremely deep state of consciousness, and is currently of little use to the hypnotist.

- 4 CPS and below (cycles per second of brainwave activity)
- Unconscious
- Not great for hypnosis or sleep
- Great for physical healing

Delusion: An irrational belief that one holds to even though it is contrary to what is evident. Someone may believe they have a love relationship with someone else even though that other person has done nothing to validate that belief.

Dentistry: Hypnosis has a long tradition in dentistry. Many dentists in the past were skilled in the use of hypnosis as an anesthetic; however hypnosis can also be used to relieve anxiety about going to the dentist. See dentistry in the chapter on waking hypnosis in this book.

Depth Scales: There are many variations on depth scales. Dave Elman held to five usable levels, one of those being waking hypnosis. Some have reduced it to three levels: light, medium and deep. The Davis-Husband uses 22 levels, while the LeCron, Bordeaux scale suggests 50 identifiable levels. Leslie LeCron has done a lot of positive work in the area of hypnosis and I'm sure a lot of research must have gone into identifying so many characteristics to so large of a scale; however the practicality of making use of such a system in a clinical practice would seem unwieldy.

The National Guild follows the six level depth scale created by Harry Arons and I feel that this is quite adequate for all practical purposes.

Depth testing or hypnotic depth tests: Simple tests given to the client by the hypnotist to determine the depth of hypnosis. Eye catalepsy and negative and positive hallucination tests are a few of the tests that help to determine trance depth. See also trance management.

Dermatillomania: See skin picking.

DID: Dissociative Identity Disorder, formerly and more commonly known as Multiple Personality Disorder. Hypnosis was the first successful method to deal with this issue and most notably by Pierre Janet. Hypnosis is still the method of choice; however this is a very involved issue and should only be worked with by a very skilled hypnotherapist.

Direct Suggestion: Not ambiguous. To the point.

Directive: A type of suggestion or style that is straight forward, to the point, even assertive. Example: "Sit back and close your eyes." See also assertive, authoritarian, and paternal.

Disguised Method: A method of inducing trance on an unwilling subject developed by Erickson and Kobie. By hypnotizing a willing subject in the presence of the unwilling subject and creating a rapport, the unwilling subject is given suggestions indirectly and hypnosis is induced.

Dissociation: was first used as a psychological term by Pierre Janet. When we use a strategy to avoid a situation or feelings we are dissociating. Day dreaming is a form of dissociation; avoidance and denial are forms of dissociation. We could also dissociate by using medications, drugs and alcohol.

We also use dissociative methods at times in hypnosis. For instance, to desensitize an overly emotional situation, we can have the client use any of a number of dissociative methods such as seeing the uncomfortable scene from a distance, or viewing the scene through a VCR while controlling the remote, or viewing the scene as if it were being acted out on a stage, etc.

Dominance-Submission relationship: In the past, less emphasis was placed on creating expectancy (waking hypnosis) and rapport, and greater reliance was placed on the subject following the operator's suggestions. Simply because the operator was placed in a more dominant role the client (submissive) followed suggestions as commanded to do so.

Double bind: We cannot maintain two opposing concepts at the same time. This is what allows different forms of catalepsy to occur. For example (once the eyes are locked tightly shut), "The harder you try to open your eyes the more difficult it becomes, try, you cannot. Try and you cannot. That's right, now relax." If the subject follows the instructions (which is necessary and is something we are checking for) then they can't simultaneously open and tighten their eyes all at the same time. This seems like a simple thing but it creates a sensation in the subject which is not usual for them. These double binds become convincers.

Downtime trance: Two types of trance are occurring simultaneously during a hypnosis session. The client is normally in a downtime trance, which means that they do not need to maintain any conscious awareness. The therapist does the managing of the session. See uptime trance.

Drama: The use of drama in hypnosis or waking hypnosis can have a positive effect. The use of drama helps to create the expectation that the desired outcome will occur.

Dream Hypnosis: an old term describing a state following a mild state of hypnosis. Probably a deep alpha state or light theta state.

DSM-IV: Diagnostic and Statistical Manual of Mental Disorders that is used by various therapists and doctors to help diagnose patients based on specific, accepted criteria. Codes in the DSM-IV are also used to code insurance claims.

Dual Induction: Also double induction. When two hypnotists are inducing the same subject at the same time, this is dual induction. The intention is for the hypnotist who is speaking into the left ear of the subject to use verbiage that is directed to the right brain while the hypnotist who is speaking into the right ear is directing language toward the left brain. Receiving different but useful information at the same time causes confusion and a likely bypass of the critical faculty so that the mind follows the instructions. This type of induction can be very quick and effective, but has the disadvantage of needing a second facilitator.

Electronic Hypnosis: Currently there are many electronic devices that can help us to use hypnosis. There are biofeedback machines that actually measure brain activity and help to achieve certain positive results. GSR (galvanic skin response) machines can do similar things as a biofeedback machine for a fraction of the cost.

Sound machines or light and sound combined can create hypnosis. Many of these types of machines include the use of binaural beats or frequencies to aid in their effectiveness.

Machines are available that have a wide selection of programs that can be used to create a large variety of positive results and can be adapted to serve large groups if necessary. An outside source can often be fed in as well to personalize a session through suggestion or to add music. Recording devices can be added to record the session for future use on some models.

These machines can be very useful in your own self hypnosis process and some hypnotists use them extensively in their professional practice. If this is the only method that a person uses in their practice then they become more of a technician than a therapist. While these machines have their place and can be useful, there is no substitute for knowing good hypnotic technique.

Elman Induction: A rapid induction developed by Dave Elman that includes depth testing and convincers built into the induction.

Embedded commands: Also embedded suggestion. A suggestion within a suggestion. The embedded command or suggestion is usually very directive and given within the text of a larger more permissive statement by creating a pause or changing the tone, etc., of the voice.

Emerging: Emerging is the term used for bringing someone out of trance. Since the client is not asleep we avoid terms like awaken although awaken has been commonly used. There are various methods for emerging someone from trance, a simple count up from one to five is most common (sometimes followed with a finger snap).

Emote: The expression of emotions.

Enuresis: Difficulty controlling the bladder, particularly at night and with children (bed wetting). Hypnosis has been quite successful with enuresis.

Ericksonian Hypnosis: Hypnotic methodology popularized by the late Milton Erickson. Some popular hallmarks of Ericksonian Hypnosis are the use of metaphor, indirect suggestion, storytelling, and the use of permissive or maternal language.

Esdaile State: This state of hypnosis is called the Esdaile state because of the work of Dr. James Esdaile. Esdaile was influenced by Elliotson's use of hypnosis for anesthesia. This is the state of hypnosis that Esdaile perfected taking the methods of Franz Anton Mesmer to a point beyond which Mesmer himself had ever achieved. Esdaile perfected this method performing thousands of surgeries using only hypnosis as an anesthesia. This state of hypnosis is still used today to perform surgeries.

The Esdaile State is characterized by sensations of the arms and legs being heavy (like lead) as well as euphoric feelings. A person cannot or will not speak or move in the Esdaile state. That may be due to the fact that it feels so good to experience this state of hypnosis that when in this state we want to maintain these good sensations and speaking or moving would only detract from the good feelings.

Some people (natural somnambulists) can enter the Esdaile (coma) state rather easily. Some stage hypnotists have experienced having a very suggestible person in the audience enter into hypnosis while he or she was focused on putting the people on stage into trance. After the show is over and everyone gets up and leaves, the hypnotist discovers a person sitting in the audience seemingly unresponsive. A lot of hypnotists have found it difficult to get such individuals out of trance and because of this some fear was raised. The fear of getting stuck in hypnosis likely came from these experiences. However, the idea that a person could get stuck in hypnosis is totally incorrect. There are ways to get a person out of this state easily, but even if nothing were done to emerge the individual he or she would eventually come out of trance on their own and get up and leave.

Exhibition (an older term): Is the public demonstration of the various degrees of hypnotism, given for amusement or scientific purposes.

Expectation: What the mind expects to happen is what tends to happen. We create an expectancy, through waking hypnosis, that a particular outcome will occur and that is what tends to happen. See also intention. Also the sections in this book on waking hypnosis and expectation.

Expectancy: What we expect to happen is what tends to happen (see waking hypnosis within this text).

Eye catalepsy: A locking down sensation of the eyelids occurs through suggestion which causes the client to feel as though they can't open their eyes. Generally this is done as a suggestibility test, but it is very much a convincer. It helps the client to notice that something different (hypnosis) is occurring and therefore they become more receptive to further suggestions. This is one example of a double bind. If the subject follows instructions they will receive the effect simply because two different things can't happen simultaneously.

Eye closure: Beginning stages of hypnosis and induction. If a client does not close their eyes when asked to do so then they are not following simple instructions which is a requirement for formal induction. Of course, people can be in hypnosis with their eyes open, and sometimes this is necessary. As a general rule, if the eyes remain open in trance for very long visual stimulus will draw the person out of trance.

Eye Fixation: A type of induction. By simply staring at a fixed point we can achieve a hypnotic trance.

Eye flutter: An indication of trance with some individuals. Not the same as REM.

Eye roll: A determination of a person's hypnotizability can be made through the eye roll process. Doctors Herbert and David Spiegel present a system by which this process works in their book *Trance and Treatment*.

Eyes open: Hypnosis achieved with the eyes open. Can be helpful in certain situations and to relieve resistance.

False Memory: The term is somewhat of a misnomer, implanted memory might be a more accurate term. Memory that is supposedly recovered during a session that may be incorrect. Usually the false memory is a projection of the therapist's beliefs (their personal agenda) into the session. If I say *see a garden of roses* to my client, their mind will take them to a garden of roses; if I say *see your father abusing you* the mind can go there as well. This is a form of leading the client and should never be a part of therapy. Families have ended up in courts and even been ruined over situations that did not occur due to the misguided encouragement of some therapists. A good deal of information is available on this topic.

Fascination: Also Donatism after Donato who popularized this method of induction and suggestion which is done by having the subject stare into the hypnotist's eyes and thereby causes the subject to mimic the movements of the hypnotist. This method may have evolved out of the old Puysegurian method done from a sitting position.

Fascination has also been used after a person has been hypnotized by then having them fixate on an object to the point that they will follow that object all around when it is moved.

Flowers Method: A simple method of induction that includes eye fixation popularized by Dr. Flowers.

Formal Hypnosis: Hypnosis performed overtly such as in a therapeutic session, but also for self hypnosis and entertainment purposes.

Forensic Hypnosis: The use of hypnosis in a legal setting such as testifying in court, the refreshment of memory for testifying purposes, and solving crimes. Specialized training and technique are required to perform forensic hypnosis.

Fractional Autohypnosis: Hypnosis of one part of the body at a time, such as in a hand or foot.

Fractionation: Re-hypnotizing a person over and over to take them deeper into hypnosis. Sometimes is referred to incorrectly as refractionation. Developed by Vogt.

Future Orientation: See mental rehearsal:

Future Progression: See mental rehearsal.

Future Pacing (also future orientation and future progression): See mental rehearsal.

Gabbling: Speeded up or nonsensical language. Often used by stage hypnotists, but also in more therapeutic hypnosis.

Gamma: A state of consciousness that is a hyper-alert, fight or flight response state. Gamma is not a very practical state for hypnotists to work in.

- Above 21 CPS to about 40 CPS (cycles per second of brainwave activity)
- State of hyper alert
- Fight or flight

Gestalt (therapy): Gestalt (the whole) is a form of therapy developed by the late Fritz Perls, Laura Perls and Paul Goodman in the 1940s – 1950s. The term gestalt has been in use in regard to psychology and form since the 1800s. Gestalt is a very imaginative process; it has been used extensively in the hypnotherapy community. It is used extensively to interact with other individuals who may or may not be on this plane and to resolve issues with them.

Giggling: A reaction that sometimes shows up at the onset of the induction. Giggling is usually caused by anxiety or uncertainty. Normally it ends as the hypnotist progresses with the session and just ignores it. There are some techniques for getting around giggling, usually a good instant induction will bypass the critical faculty and it is over.

Glove anesthesia: Glove anesthesia has been around for a long time. By creating anesthesia in a hand we can then transfer that anesthesia through suggestion and physical movement of the hand to some other area of the body. One easy way to do this is to have the client imagine that the hand is in a bucket of ice or ice water and suggesting the numbing sensations that come with that. Once the client has achieved numbness in their hand then it can be transferred to some other part of the body. This process can also be considered to be a convincer. Once the subject notices and experiences the different sensations the acceptance of further suggestions becomes more likely. Achieving a state of somnambulism is necessary for anesthesia to occur.

Guided Meditation: Another form of hypnosis which usually involves some simple type of induction such as a progressive relaxation. It is commonly done with groups or individuals and with some sort of goal in mind. Similar to a guided visualization.

Guided Visualization or Guided Imagery: Taking and individual or group on a specific visual type of hypnotic journey. This method can be used to aid in stress relief, healing, spirituality, etc.

Habit: An action or condition that has become involuntary through repetition. Habits are a subconscious mind activity and therefore hypnosis can work well to remove or establish a habit. Once we establish an action to become a habit it takes very little effort to maintain that action. Habits can work for or against us. For instance, when we get up in the morning we brush our teeth without giving it a thought just because that is what we always do. And that is a good habit.

We might go to the same fast food place every day and that has become a habit; however the negative effects of that dietary choice may be working against us. Through hypnosis we can change a habit and even replace it with a new, healthier habit (going to the gym regularly), and even without having to go through all of the repetition.

Hallucination: See positive and negative hallucination.

Hand levitation: Much like forms of catalepsy, hand levitation can be a suggestibility test, convincer, or help to determine trance depth.

Hand passes (also, passes): Mesmer may be responsible for this type of hypnotic induction which incorporates the passing of hands over the body.

As Mesmer began to distance himself from the use of physical magnets he felt that he possessed magnetism within his very being, and that he could project that magnetism to his clients (who lacked appropriate magnetism due to their illness) and cause them to heal. Not unlike the laying on of hands, but more likely Mesmer was producing a hypnotic trance just through the expectancy that he created. In later times it was used more for theatrical purposes.

Handshake induction: This is an induction made popular by Dave Elman whereby he used three shakes of the hand, each shake taking the subject deeper into hypnosis. Variations of this method were popularized by Milton Erickson and Gil Boyne. I enjoy using it as taught by Gil Boyne where one handshake becomes an instant induction.

Hetero Hypnosis: Hypnosis performed with another such as a hypnotist, as opposed to self hypnosis which is done alone. This term is not common nowadays.

Homework assignments (action plans): Tasks given to the client to help integrate their therapy into their normal daily lives.

Heightened Selectivity: In hypnosis it may serve us to be more focused on one thing (the hypnotist's voice) than another (potentially distracting work going on outside). In hypnosis, even though we experience heightened sensory awareness, we are able to blot out those things that do not serve us in the moment.

Heightened Suggestibility (also hyper-suggestibility): In some states of consciousness (theta for instance) we are more receptive to suggestions than in other states (beta).

Highway Hypnosis: Hypnotic effects that occur while driving. Hypnosis occurs while driving for a number of reasons. See the chapter *What Else is Hypnosis* under driving.

Hyper-emperia: Using hypnotic process to go up in consciousness rather than down.

Hypermnesia: Vivid memory and recollection, the opposite of amnesia. Can also become a defense mechanism adopted by young children who carry it on through adulthood. Also a form of regression to enhance details of a situation.

Hypersuggestibility: A state of heightened suggestibility. Some people are naturally more suggestible or hypnotizable than others. Also, when we are in a state of somnambulism we are much more suggestible. We are also more suggestible when there is a bypass of the critical faculty.

Hypnarcotherapist: An ambiguous and—prior to this writing—never before used term that implies that your hypnotist has fallen asleep.

Hypnoanalysis: Basically early terminology for age regression type work. Hadfield is credited for originating this term. During World Wars I and II and the Korean War many soldiers were suffering from "shell shock" or battle neurosis (what would be more likely referred to as PTSD nowadays). A lack of psychiatrists at the time prompted a search for quicker, easier methods of treatment which prompted the successful use of hypnosis to work with these sufferers.

Hypno-anesthesia: Achieving total loss of feeling sensation in some area or areas of the body through the use of hypnosis. While still in use today, using hypnosis to create anesthesia was more popular in the days prior to the advent of modern chemical anesthetics.

HypnoBirthing': Is a registered trade mark of the Mongan Method of hypnotic child birth. There are many such practitioners who use different forms of easy or painless childbirth. Some methods make use of deep hypnosis like the Esdaile State, while others use lighter states of hypnosis. The positive effects can be achieved through a number of different approaches. The term *hypnobirthing* has become synonymous with any usage of hypnosis and childbirth.

Hypnodrama: Playing out a role in hypnosis that parallels the client's conflict.

Hypnologic, hypnology, hypnologist: The study of sleep and hypnosis.

Hypnotic Ablation: A technique of hypnotic regression (not common).

Hypnotic Child birth: See Birth by Hypnosis™, Painless Childbirth, HypnoBirthing.

Hypnotic Coma: See coma state.

Hypnotic Delivery: Older terminology for Hypnosis for birthing. Was often done in the Esdaile state.

HypnoFertility: HypnoFertility is a registered trademark of the hypnotic methods of achieving fertility through the process developed by Lynsi Eastburn. It is the subject of her book *It's Conceivable! Hypnosis for Fertility*. Using hypnosis to resolve fertility issues has been around for some time.

Hypno-disc (also hypnotron): A spiral type of spinning disk that has been around for a long time and is used to hypnotize. Sometimes it is referred to as the Braid fascination technique.

Hypnogogic (also Hypnagogia or Hypnogagia): A hypnotic state that we experience when going off to sleep.

Hypno-Junkie: A non-technical term for someone who has discovered the joys of hypnosis.

Hypnoidal: Early signs of hypnosis including relaxation, drowsiness, fluttering of the eyelids, closing of the eyes, mental relaxation.

Hypnopompic: Hypnotic experiences that occur when transitioning from sleep to a wakeful state.

Hypnosis: This term was first used by Dr. James Braid during the nineteenth century; the word hypnosis is Greek for sleep. Braid realized that he wasn't actually dealing with sleep and tried to change the name to monoideism, but the word hypnosis had already caught on.

Hypnosis attached to sleep: According to Elman, sleep achieved by giving someone a post hypnotic suggestion that they will fall asleep instantly on cue.

Hypnosleep: While Elman believed you couldn't create sleep from the hypnotic state without using post hypnotic suggestion, the reverse was not the same. A person that is asleep could be given hypnotic suggestions and then returned to sleep. Elman gave precise steps to achieve this process.

Hypnotherapist: The terms hypnotist and hypnotherapist are often used interchangeably. There is a distinction, however, and it tends to be more in application and level of skill. While most any hypnotist could create some positive therapeutic results with their hypnosis skills, a hypnotherapist should be someone whose main focus is that of helping others through hypnotic therapeutic methods.

A stage hypnotist may be very skilled in the use of hypnosis for entertainment purposes and not be very talented at helping people with emotional issues. Although from personal experience, those worlds and methods can transfer well. Some of the finest hypnotherapists of our time were stage hypnotists originally. On the other hand, there are people who do hypnosis and are capable of helping a lot of people with basic issues, but are not qualified to (or are regulated in their area so that they are unable to) do more involved therapeutic work.

On the flip side of that there are people doing hypnotherapy who have very limited skills in the area of hypnotism. In my opinion it is important to have a strong foundation in good hypnosis skills before entering into more involved or therapeutic practices. Without a good foundation in the fundamentals the therapist could be using a cannon when a fly swatter is all that is necessary.

U.S.A definition for Hypnotherapist:

The U.S. (Department of Labor) Directory of Occupational Titles (D.O.T. 079.157.010) supplies the following definition.

"Hypnotherapist" – Induces hypnotic state in client to increase motivation or alter behavior patterns through hypnosis. Consults with client to determine the nature of problem. Prepares client to enter hypnotic states by explaining how hypnosis works and what the client will experience. Tests subject to determine degrees of physical and emotional suggestibility.

Induces hypnotic state in client using individualized methods and techniques of hypnosis based on interpretation of test results and analysis of client's problem. May train client in self-hypnosis conditioning.

Hypnotherapy: Excerpt from NGH via Rev. Dr. C. Scot Giles: While the Guild still considers the words "hypnotism" and "hypnotherapy" to be synonyms, increasingly a distinction is emerging in which "hypnotism" is understood as a non-therapeutic practice of the hypnotic arts and sciences, while "hypnotherapy" refers to psychotherapy by means of hypnotism. This distinction is encouraged by the Guild. *The entire statement is too lengthy to include here, but deserves your further attention. Check the Guild web site (www.ngh.net) or the Eastburn site: www.hypnodenver.com.*

Hypnotic Coma: See the Esdaile state.

Hypnotic Language: While it may seem that the hypnotist is not saying anything differently than someone would expect to hear, subtle differences in language can have a big effect on the subconscious. Sometimes the hypnotic language is not grammatically correct; for instance, we may use tenses that would seem incorrect at times. However the hypnotic or subconscious effect is what counts.

Hypnotic Lock: A belief that one hypnotist can give and individual a suggestion that no other hypnotist will be able to hypnotize them. This notion would seem to fly in the face of the client being in control and the hypnotist not being able to give the subject unacceptable suggestions. Even if a subject were to accept a hypnotic lock it wouldn't take much for a skilled hypnotist to break it.

Hypnotic Mask: The appearance of relaxed facial muscles when someone is in deep hypnosis.

Hypnotic Passes: The hands of the hypnotist passing by the subject's head or body to induce a trance state. This type of induction was common in the early days of hypnosis and was used by Mesmer and others.

Hypnotism: The non-therapeutic use of hypnosis such as sports enhancement, stress reduction, study skills, etc. See Hypnotherapy.

Hypnotist: The person (sometimes known as the operator) who is facilitating the use of hypnosis which could be for clinical, experimental or entertainment purposes. See also hypnotherapist.

Hypnotizability: In the past different beliefs and statistics have been stated as to who and how hypnotizable people are. The fact is that every normal, high functioning individual is hypnotizable. While there may be some merit to different theories and studies, when it comes to therapeutic hypnosis most anyone can be a good subject. And, of course, the skill of the therapist can help to ensure positive results for most anyone.

Stage hypnosis has helped to create the notion that only certain people will make good hypnotic subjects, and for stage purposes I would agree. However someone who might not perform well in an entertainment setting may do great in a more therapeutic setting.

Hypnotron: See hypno-disc.

Hypno-vision or HypnoVision: The use of hypnosis to improve vision. Apparently we are not locked into popular beliefs about being born with vision issues or that the eyes must get worse in time. My father wore glasses all of his adult life, but his vision improved with age and with no effort on his part. By the time he was in his 80s his prescription was so low he could do without his glasses most of the time. I improved my own eyesight as a youngster through the use of eye exercises. A friend of mine wore coke bottle glasses and started doing the eye exercises and by the end of the school year he had thrown his glasses away. Lisette Scholl (HypnoVision Westwood Publishing 1997) puts hypnosis to use for improving vision and what the author has to say makes a great deal of sense.

Hysteria: Charcot described hypnosis as a state of hysteria. Hysteria was the main concern of early therapists such as Freud. They believed psychological issues were female. It's not hard to imagine how male-oriented and dominated thinking was in those days, and so a lot of attention was given to explaining these bizarre behaviors in women. Nowadays we understand gender differences more and accept that everyone (male or female) has emotional needs that can be helped through therapy. No matter how awkward these early attempts at psychotherapy might seem, it laid the ground work for methods that have been the savior for many.

Ideomotor signaling (also ideomotor response): A type of interaction between the client and therapist where verbalizing is not used. Signals are established prior to and/or during trance that will allow the client to communicate, usually through the wiggling of fingers. Communication is limited to yes or no questions. Verbalizing tends to engage the conscious mind and will either lighten the trance state or create more ambiguity through the engagement of the conscious mind. The ideomotor response becomes a direct response of the subconscious. This type of hypnotic work was developed by David B. Cheek.

Implied directives: By using an indirect suggestion we can create another more direct effect. It is somewhat similar to an embedded suggestion although without the changes in voice. Example; "When you notice the temperature change in a moment, you will sink twice as deep."

Imprinting: Behavior evoked through great physical or emotional stress. Usually occurs very early in life and may be the cause of an ISE or what some might refer to as a core issue.

Induction: A method of formally assisting someone into a state of hypnosis. The induction can be performed by a trained hypnotist on an individual or a group. An individual can do their own induction on themselves as part of their own self hypnosis process. An informal type of induction occurs when we find ourselves staring off into space or perhaps watching a flickering flame, etc.

Indirect Hypnosis: Covert hypnosis, hypnosis produced without the subject being aware. Milton Erickson's disguised method would be an example of indirect hypnosis.

Indirect Suggestion: Suggestions that allow the client to interpret them in their own way. Indirect suggestions can be covert and unobtrusive and may not deal directly with the client's issue. Example: "I wonder about my high school graduation, perhaps you wonder about your high school graduation at times." Indirect suggestions can take in a wide range of suggestions including ambiguous suggestions, puns, embedded suggestions, metaphors, etc.

Informal Trance: Trance entered into without the aid of a hypnotist and often without the individual's awareness of going into the state. Highway hypnosis or staring into the flames of a campfire or candle would be examples of informal trance.

Informed Child: In inner child and regression therapy the informed child is the child that due to time and history has become able to understand the cause for certain events (traumas) and thereby understand those issues.

Inner Child: Therapeutic work that has been popularized by John Bradshaw and has been embraced in hypnotherapeutic process by many.

Instant Induction: An induction that is instantaneous. The bypass of the critical faculty is achieved, usually through some form of misdirection (possibly causing a startle response). A subject can actually go directly into a somnambulistic state, however the hypnotist must continue to maintain hypnotic patter so that the subject will remain hypnotized.

Intake (also pretalk): The part of the session before the hypnosis occurs which includes determining the session intention, gathering client history, educating the client about hypnosis, addressing the client's concerns and questions, and suggestibility testing.

Intention: What we intend to have happen often is the result. We create an intention during the intake portion (waking hypnosis), as well as in the trance state, that a particular outcome will occur. See also expectation.

Interactive Process: Occurs during hypnosis when the therapist talks to the client and the client responds verbally. Also see ideomotor signaling.

Interspersal of Suggestions: Repetition of key words and phrases throughout a series of suggestions.

ISE: The Initial Sensitizing Event. Literally the very first time an emotion (trauma) was triggered that is now causing an emotional problem in the client's life. Also see imprint.

Karma: The collection of samskara (experiences) that one accrues which can travel from one life to the next and is both positive and negative. If this process is correct then we can have an effect on this karma through certain hypnotic procedures.

Key Word or Key Phrases: Words or phrases that are repeated that pertain to the desired results. It could be something simple like "relax" or "relax now" or it could be something more involved that has to do with the client's goal. Key words or phrases can be part of self hypnosis as a conditioner or they could be gleaned from a client's intake by the hypnotist and repeated later in trance.

Kinesthetic Anchors: A physical association (such as touch) to an emotional feeling creates a kinesthetic anchor. For instance, once a client achieves positive emotional sensations in trance, simply having them touch a place on the body (particularly the location associated with the positive feelings) creates a kinesthetic anchor which we can make use of at a later time (see triggers).

Kinesthetic: Physical and emotional feeling. Also a sensory orientation, as some people may predominantly experience their environment visually or through auditory or even olfactory sensations. Others are kinesthetic and experience and learn in a feeling mode. Kinesthetic people will learn more easily through a hands-on approach or by intuition.

Kinesthetic Disorientation: By manipulating the body, especially the head, a sense of disorientation, confusion and discomfort occurs. A bypass of the critical factor occurs and a desire to make sense of what is occurring causes the subject to follow the suggestions of the hypnotist so as to take the subject into trance or to accept suggestions.

Lacrimation: Tearing or increased tearing of the eyes. Often we notice a tear that forms at the corner of the eye that is an indication of hypnotic trance.

Law of Reversed Effect: Even if a subject consciously resists hypnosis, they will eventually find it difficult to stay cognizant and will drift into a hypnotic state. This law, initiated by Emile Coué, states that expectation of a sensation (whether it is desired or not) tends to bring on that sensation due to imagination being stronger than will power. The harder one tries to do something (using will power) the more difficult it becomes. Having continual negative thoughts will bring them into realization. The harder we try to fall asleep, or remember a name, the more difficult it becomes.

Law of Dominant Effect: Recognized by Frederick Pierce, a follower of Coué, a strong emotion tends to replace a weaker one. Aversion methods take advantage of this law.

Lay Hypnotist: A term which is sometimes used to describe someone who is not a professional hypnotist such as a hobbyist, or someone who uses hypnosis as an adjunct to other work. Many therapists who are trained in other methods of psychotherapy have had some short course in hypnosis, but are not skilled in its use, or use it only occasionally and are, therefore, lay hypnotists.

Laying on of hands: Dates back to the time of the bible and is not dissimilar to the *Royal Touch*. Even today, being touched by the Pope or some other holy person is considered to have special healing powers. Basically the expectancy that is created causes the hypnosis (believability).

Leading: Normally leading is something we as hypnotists want to avoid. If a therapist leads the client, such as during a regression, the likely outcome will be only a pseudoregression. Leading would be for the therapist to say something like, "Is your father there in this new scene beating you again?" Instead of a non-leading question such as, "What's happening now?"

There are times when we can use leading and it is appropriate, such as when doing a guided visualization, either with a group or individually. We may want to create a group exercise where everyone is having a similar experience or we may be leading a client or a group through a healing process in the body, etc., and in these types of situations leading is more appropriate. Certainly leading cannot take place at all in a Forensic Hypnosis session.

Leading Statements: See pacing and leading.

LeCron, Bordeaux Scale: A hypnosis depth scale that identifies 50 different levels.

Lethargy: Beginning stages of hypnosis, a term first applied to hypnosis by Charcot.

Leverage Techniques: Techniques or suggestions that tend to be accepted because there is a power differential. When the mind notices that one choice is more appealing than the other it tends to choose the more appealing option. See crossroads and sandwich technique.

Life purpose regression: It has become popular of late for people to find out what their purpose was for coming into their current life. It is believed that by taking a person back to the time just after their most recent incarnation and just prior to this life time we can gain the information on our life purpose. World renowned author and speaker Dr. Wayne Dyer describes a life purpose regression he had with a hypnotherapist in his book *Inspiration*.

Lucid Dreaming: Basically dreams that we take control of. Now, if we are taking control in a dream, wouldn't that mean that the conscious mind would have to be at least just a teeny bit present? Could it be that lucid dreaming is a sort of self hypnosis?

Lucid Sleep: A term applied to animal magnetism by José Custodio de Faria which would be an early term for hypnosis.

Magnetic Sleep: While passing magnets over an ill person Pusegur (1784) noticed that the person went into a state that was not either a sleep state or a waking state. He discovered this the same time as Mesmer was being discredited by the medical commission. Of course, we now know this state to be hypnosis.

Mantras: Repetitious (sacred) words or phrases that help to focus the mind away from conscious thoughts, and to achieve a trance state (hypnosis), usually for spiritual purposes.

Manual compounding: Tying verbal suggestion to physical cues. By using physical manipulation we can compound the verbal suggestion. Each time I touch your forehead you sink deeper into hypnosis. The Elman arm drop can and has been used in this manner.

Mass Hypnosis: Hypnosis that occurs in large numbers, such as an entire country. See waking hypnosis in this book.

Master Hypnotist: Despite what it would seem to indicate, Master Hypnotist is a term used by some organizations to acknowledge entry level hypnosis certification.

Matching: A rapport building strategy originated by Dr. Milton Erickson. By assuming similar body posture to our clients (or others) we begin to create a rapport with that individual. Some people refer to it as mirroring, but we aren't actually doing the exact same posture as the other individual.

Maternal: Permissive suggestion or style associated with the mothering or female style. This type of suggestion or style was popularized by Milton Erickson. See also permissive.

Mayo Clinic: One of the earliest major medical facilities in this country to embrace hypnosis. Dave Elman trained the Mayo Clinic anesthesiologists in the use of hypnosis and soon the Mayo Clinic became the place to go for surgery. The Mayo Clinic is still one of the very best medical facilities. It is a big supporter of hypnosis and has plenty of information available on its website.

Meditation: Meditation covers a wide range of methodology and theory. Meditation has a wide range of purpose and usefulness. It is a way of tapping into the subconscious and putting some purpose to it. Meditation is an application of hypnosis.

Mental Rehearsal: Moving the client ahead in trance to the present or future. This aids in determining if the work we have done has been successful, and/or as a tool to enable the client to see how their life will be if their present strategy continues or a new strategy is adopted.

Mesmeric Coma: See Esdaile state.

Mesmeric Method: A method of inducing trance that includes hand passes and may be followed by a test for arm catalepsy to ensure success.

Mesmerism: An old term for hypnosis which came from the days of Franz Anton Mesmer, who may be the first modern hypnotist. The term mesmerism or mesmerized is still in use today.

Metaphor: Therapeutic stories or analogies that are meant to elicit and guide the client's internal associations. Metaphors are one form of indirect suggestion that can have multiple functions and are useful to address a problem theme the metaphor can parallel. Metaphors are non-threatening and engaging because they are only indirectly related to the issue.

Metaphysical Hypnosis: Hypnosis is metaphysical by nature; however some styles of hypnosis take it to the sublime by incorporating things like spirit guides, shamanic ritual, angels, white light, etc.

Metronome Method: A method of induction using a metronome popularized by Watkins.

Middle of nowhere technique: A technique created by Milton Erickson to create dissociation in the client, thereby creating a separation and different perspective allowing for change.

Mild Hypnosis: an early term for light state (alpha) state. The subject has good awareness, but is more suggestible.

Mind Control: This is a huge topic and some definitions say that it is not to be confused with brain washing. Others compare them closely which seems reasonable, although mind control seems to have much more negative applications associated with it.

Many things can and are applied through mind control including but not limited to: control of information, social and physical environment, manipulation, sacred ideology which is above question. Common words or phrases may be given totally different meanings so that outsiders will not understand what is actually being said and lots more.

Misdirection: By leading the mind in one direction, and then taking off in a totally different direction, we cause misdirection. This can bypass the critical factor for the purpose of instant induction or implanting suggestions.

Monoideism: After James Braid coined the term hypnosis (Greek for sleep) he realized that it was not actually sleep and he tried to change the name to monoideism (single-idea-ism), however the term hypnosis had taken hold (and is much catchier).

Multiple Personality Disorder: See DID.

Myoclonic Jerk: The involuntary jerking of one's muscles usually noticed when falling off to sleep. Sometimes the jerking sensations are associated with a startle and can even cause a person to sit up. These jerking movements are not uncommon in hypnosis and are not generally of any concern. Some hypnotists are concerned that the trance has ended—especially if the client sits up—but that is not the case, other than in those times when the client may be startled out of trance. The client can quickly be re-inducted as necessary.

Myths: There are many myths connected to hypnosis. See the section on myths within this text.

Nail Biting (Onychophagia): Compulsive biting or chewing at the fingernails and/or the surrounding skin, cuticles etc. A body focused repetitive behavior or impulse control disorder. Hypnosis can be very effective for nail biting.

Nancy Method: A method of induction that includes staring at two of the hypnotist's fingers, while suggestions of becoming sleepy are given in a monotonous tone.

Nancy School of Hypnosis: A famous school of hypnosis in Nancy, France which was formed by Ambroise A. Liebealt and Hippolyte Bernhiem, who was a professor at the Nancy School of Medicine. Many of the early names in hypnosis are associated with both the Nancy school and the Salpêtrière school, including Sigmund Freud.

Natural Method: a type of emergence whereby the client is allowed to be left alone until they naturally come back to a normal state of consciousness. This method is not often used since the subject is now in charge and the hypnotist needs to get on to the next client.

Negative Hallucination: Not seeing something that is present. We can evaluate someone's trance depth based on their ability to create a negative hallucination.

Negative suggestions: Work in a sort of reverse psychology. The hypnotist can cause a response by suggesting that the client not respond. Examples: "Don't think of the Eiffel Tower." "There is no need to think about how good you really feel." "Don't even consider exercising after work."

The way the mind works we must think about something in order to not think about it. We can't just not consider something that is mentioned (whew).

Neurosis: Functional mental health disorders such as depression, phobias, anxiety, compulsive disorders, etc. Hypnosis can be a good choice for these kinds of issues.

Neurypnology: Nervous sleep. Dr. James Braid wrote on this topic which included his ideas on hypnosis. He stated that hypnosis could be more easily produced by fixating the eyes up rather than straight ahead. This was the beginning of hypnosis being accepted by the medical community in the 1840's.

NGH: The National Guild of Hypnotists is the oldest, largest, and most prestigious hypnosis certification organization in the world.

NLP: Nuerolinguistic Programming is a therapeutic methodology developed by Richard Bandler and John Grinder. It utilizes what are basically methods of hypnosis in a more cognitive state. NLP was based on the work of Milton Erickson, Fritz Perls, and Virginia Satire—primarily Milton Erickson.

Nocebo: Latin for "I will harm." The nocebo effect is a kind of an opposite effect of the placebo. Nocebo is when we experience an unwanted effect that is not present in that substance. For instance, during a placebo study, if the person receiving the placebo thinks they are getting the actual medication, they may also experience the negative side effects that are associated with that medication (the nocebo). The nocebo can be thought of as a sort of psychosomatic response. See the chapter *Placebo Effect* in this book.

Non-conscious mind: A term currently used by some to describe what we refer to as the sub-conscious mind. It is felt by some that sub-conscious implies that part of the mind is beneath the conscious mind, implying it is of less importance so the term non-conscious is felt to be a better choice. Who knows if this term will gain greater acceptance, however once a term like sub-conscious becomes cliché it tends to remain common. James Braid tried to change the name of hypnosis to *monoideism,* but hypnosis had already caught on. Even though the term Multiple Personality Disorder has been changed to *Dissociative Identity Disorder* (DID) the origin term is still the most commonly used.

Non-verbal Induction: Trance achieved without the spoken word. Lots of things can take us into trance without someone speaking to us. Just observing others in trance causes us to want to do the same. Placing a hand on the shoulder or using a trigger that has been previously anchored can be a non-verbal induction. The aura induction is a good non-verbal induction that can easily be demonstrated. See also highway hypnosis or driving.

Non-verbal Suggestion: Suggestions given without speaking. A look, a glance, a raised eyebrow, pointing or handing an object to someone are non-verbal suggestions. The egg on the front of this book is a non-verbal suggestion.

Numeric Amnesia: Causing numbers to disappear is a popular way to determine if somnambulism has been achieved and can be a crowd pleaser for demonstration or entertainment purposes.

Open-eyed Somnambulism: A deep state of hypnosis achieved with the eyes open. Has proven to be useful particularly in certain medical applications.

Operator: A term that has become less common but describes the person who is doing the hypnosis (hypnotist, hypnotherapist) to someone else (subject).

Pacing Chain: Creating a long series of pacing statements leads the client into a very accepting space. What I refer to as leading the mind down the merry path. Few, if any, leading statements are required. See also Pacing and Leading.

Pace Current Experience: a simpler version of Pacing and Leading, making use of Utilization in the context of a shorter statement.

Pacing and Leading: Pacing and leading is a process of giving a series of statements to the client. The rule of thumb is three pacing statements followed by a leading statement, though that is not set in stone. Pacing statements are highly believable truisms. These pacing statements are easy for the mind to accept and difficult to refute. The leading statement is the statement that may be a bit less believable but helps us to move the client in the direction we need to go. This is very much what, in sales, is referred to as a yes set. Each pacing statement that leads to a yes answer will cause the mind to continue to give a yes answer (which leads the customer to the eventual "yes I will sign on the dotted line").

Example: You might notice the sound of the ventilation system when it comes on. You might notice the sounds of people in the building. You might notice a phone ringing in another office. *And any of these sounds will take you deeper and deeper into relaxation.* You might notice sounds coming from the outside like, traffic or the weather. You might notice me taking notes. You might notice me shuffling papers. And *any of these sounds will take you deeper and deeper into relaxation.*

The first three statements are the pacing statements; their believability makes these statements easy for the mind to accept. Based on the acceptance of those first three pacing statements the mind is more inclined to accept the last statement (italicized), the leading statement. The leading statement is where we want the client to end up (relaxed in this example). This example of pacing and leading is also an example of sounds patter or utilization.

Pain: Hypnosis can be very useful in the relief of pain. Pain is a signal from the body that something is wrong and something needs to be done. Medical attention and testing needs to be done before we use hypnotic pain relief methods. It may be easy to get rid of headaches, for instance, with hypnosis; however it is important that we determine the cause first. If the client has a brain tumor, that must be addressed first. Also see painted words.

Painless Childbirth: The use of hypnosis to create a pain free childbirth. This type of hypnotic childbirth normally makes use of the Esdaile state of hypnosis.

Painted Words: Emotionally charged words that describe the client's symptoms directly such as: pain, headache, fear, anxiety, impotence, heights, exam, etc.

In hypnosis we avoid using these words that describe the client's issue directly. If the therapist uses the painted word then we are bringing attention to the very thing that we wish to be free of. If my client wants to be rid of the Eiffel Tower, I need to avoid referring directly to the Eiffel Tower. Each time I refer to the Eiffel Tower the mind has to create that. If I say "Don't think of the Eiffel Tower" what happens? In order to not think of something we have to think about it. It's like a computer, the words Eiffel Tower may never have popped up on the computer screen before now, but once we enter the words Eiffel Tower the computer begins searching data banks about the Eiffel Tower. As hypnotists we can suggest things like, "Old, unwanted memories just slip away," and by doing so we have never mentioned memories of the Eiffel Tower.

Also, we can substitute other words that are less charged than the painted words such as *sensations* instead of pain. Avoiding painted words at the end of the session is very important as well. If I said after the session, "Now, how is that headache" or "is your headache gone?" I have just recreated that there is a headache present and I have sent the client on a mission to find it. And it is likely that they will.

Parts Therapy: A type of hypnotic therapy whereby problems can be resolved by working (talking) with different aspects of the self. While this type of parts integration work was popularized by the late Charles Tebbetts, it has been around for quite some time. Janet, Charcot, and Bruer made reference to it, as did Carl Jung. Before any of them there was Asagioli.

Parts therapy can be an effective way of dealing with inner conflict or used for decision making purposes. Tebbetts's protégé, Roy Hunter, has written excellent material in this area.

Passes: see hand passes.

Past Life Regression: A type of hypnosis that takes people into previous lifetimes to resolve issues with, or to have a positive influence on, their current life (or for entertainment purposes). There are different opinions as to whether past lives actually exist or not, and to whether or not they are just subconscious metaphors for issues in the client's life. However, it is advised that a good hypnotist have knowledge and skill in this area in order to effectively facilitate a client's process as may become necessary. Spontaneous past life regression can and does sometimes occur. See also karma.

Paternal: Suggestions or style which is direct, authoritarian, more characteristically male in style.

Patter: The repetitious language used by hypnotists, spiel, shtick or written or memorized scripts.

Pavlovian Response: Ivan Pavlov developed or popularized the theory of conditioned response by causing dogs to salivate when he rang a bell. See conditioned response.

Permissive: Softer, less directive suggestions or style. Associated with the maternal. Example, "Whenever you feel like it you might want to sit back and close your eyes." Permissive suggestions and style are associated with Milton Erickson however Erickson was neither permissive nor authoritarian. He utilized whatever style was best suited for the moment.

Pharsing: A tendency for the mind to miss the true meaning of a statement by focusing only on those words that the mind finds to be important. This tendency occurs when words having a not derivative are used, such as can't, don't, couldn't, wouldn't, shouldn't, etc. For instance, in the following sentence: *don't forget your book*. The mind tends to not notice the *don't* part of the sentence and just hears *forget your book*. As a result, we often get exactly the response we didn't want. It is best to avoid statements using words of a not derivative and especially when giving hypnotic suggestions. However, we can cause this phenomenon to work in our favor as well. For example, if I were to say: *don't think about all the fun you could have while camping*, what has happened is that the mind is now thinking about having fun camping. This actually works well if my intention was for you to have fun camping.

Be aware when taking an exam. Questions that contain words of a not derivative are among those questions we are most likely to get wrong even though we know the correct answer to the question.

Pharsing also is no doubt a product of transderivational search which means that when we try to make meaning out of words we convert those words into the experience which is connected with those words. In essence, we tend to imagine the very thing that we are trying to avoid.

Pharsing also occurs with visual cues. The not smoking sign with an X through it does not cause someone to not want to smoke. *Don't* signs of any type with the big X through them only bring attention to that thing that we desire to not have happen.

Phobia: A compulsive and persistent fear. We all naturally have some fears: for instance having some fear of heights would be normal, but to not be able to step off the curb or climb the stairs is crippling. Hypnosis is the quickest and most effective method of eliminating phobias. See *The Power of the Past*.

Physical Method: (emerging) there are many methods to physically emerge a subject from trance, including, blowing on the eyelids, opening the eyelids with force, sprinkling cold water, rubbing the eyelids, using a sharp sound (finger snap) etc.. This was done more in the past and should be a back up method rather than primary.

Placebo: Latin for "I will please." An inert substance presented to have healing powers or to be a medication which it is not. Also it is a study using inert substances to compare the effectiveness of a non-placebo. See also nocebo and the chapter in this book *The Placebo Effect*.

Plenary Trance: A stuporous condition in which all spontaneous activity is inhibited. Leslie Le Cron and Erickson refer to it as a state of physical and mental lethargy, deeper than we would consider somnambulism. Plenary trance is the deepest state shown on the Le Cron Bordeaux depth scale of fifty.

Point of Reference: A previous time that the subject experienced sensations that we can use to encourage the client in a positive direction. For instance, if the client is going in to take an important exam we can, as part of their hypnotic process, take them back to a time when they had an experience of doing really well on an exam. We can revivify that early scene and reintegrate the good feelings and sensations from the earlier experience to create the new test taking situation.

We could use a negative experience to the client's benefit in a similar way. For instance, we could take someone back to a time (point of reference) when cigarettes tasted horrible (such as the first time they ever smoked) and associate the awful feelings and sensations that they had experienced earlier with awful sensations to be associated with smoking from now on.

Positive Hallucination: Seeing something that isn't there. (See negative hallucination). While we tend to think of hallucinations as a visual thing we can also experience hallucinations of taste, smell, temperature and sounds. When a client achieves positive or negative hallucinations in trance it is an indication of trance depth.

Positive Suggestions: Are a very common type of suggestions and somewhat self explanatory. Positive suggestions are not limited to one tightly defined type of suggestion, but more so to any suggestion that would elicit a positive response which could be a direct suggestion, embedded, metaphor, ambiguous, etc. Positive suggestions are often given in the form of an affirmation. *Every day in every way you are better and better.*

Post Hypnotic Amnesia: Amnesia for what transpired during the hypnosis session. This can be triggered by the suggestion of the hypnotist or can occur spontaneously. This phenomenon was first noted by Philippe François Deleuze and the Marquis de Puysegar around 1784. Using posthypnotic amnesia was popular among some hypnotists who believed it would help when things of an emotional nature were uncovered in trance. Often stage hypnotists will give subjects a suggestion that they won't recall some or any of the things that they did on stage. Some stage subjects will spontaneously experience posthypnotic amnesia, perhaps to avoid the embarrassment of explaining things that they said or did or because they believe that the amnesia is a normal outcome.

Posthypnotic Response: The response that occurs in the client's real world as a result of the posthypnotic suggestion.

Post Hypnotic Suggestion: Suggestions given during the hypnosis session that will produce a positive result later on after the session. "When you arrive at your classroom desk to take your final exam you notice these same confident feelings that you notice right this very moment."

Postural sway: A type of preliminary exercise (suggestibility test). It is more advanced than eye catalepsy or Chevreul's pendulum and should be treated that way. The backward postural sway and its variations are most common, and then the forward postural sway. It can be taken right into a hypnotic induction.

Post-hypnotism or Post-Suggestion: Early terms for posthypnotic suggestion.

Prayer: When done with the proper intention prayer becomes a trance state (hypnosis). Refer to the chapter *What Else is Hypnosis.*

Preoperative attitude: The waking hypnosis prior to a surgical procedure. Of course we want that to be the most positive possible. Elman suggested not performing surgery on someone who had a poor preoperative attitude.

Presuppositions: A suggestion that assumes that an outcome will occur; when it will occur may be somewhat ambiguous. Example: "It will be nice to experience how it feels when you understand everything in this book."

Pre-talk or pre-induction talk: See intake.

Pretend Method (also act as if): See rehearsal method.

Proe-hypnotic Suggestion: (From General Techniques of Hypnotism, Wietzenhoffer.) It is the converse of a posthypnotic suggestion and operates essentially through the same mechanism. That is, one can give a waking suggestion which is to become effective upon or during the first (or some other) occasion the subject is hypnotized. When subsequently the subject is hypnotized, no further suggestion is given. Being in the hypnotic state seems to act as a catalyst for the waking suggestion. Introduced by Stembo.

Process Suggestions: Are suggestions that are less detailed or specific and let the client fill in their own details. For instance, instead of specifically describing in detail a relaxing scene for my client I might just say, "Imagine yourself anywhere that causes you to feel relaxed."

Progressive relaxation: A very common slow type of induction that focuses on progressively relaxing individual muscle groups throughout the body one at a time.

Propaganda: Messages given to influence large numbers of people. Propaganda is not necessarily an evil thing, but often works off of not giving the whole picture or lying by omission. During the cold war we heard a lot about Russian propaganda, but how much of that was just propaganda of our own. Certainly advertising can be a form of propaganda. Advertisers remind us of the wonderful things that their product can do for us, but they never seem to tell us that you could get better results some other or cheaper way. Propaganda has a way of luring us into a kind of hypnosis where we want to believe what we hear.

Pseudo-regression: Not a true regression (sham). Usually occurs when the therapist leads their client rather than aiding the client to come to their own realizations, or when the client is not in deep enough in trance and/ or has too much conscious mind involvement.

Psychological Method: (emerge) this type of method includes telling the client that at a certain moment they will be out of trance. Usually a count from 1 to 3 or 1 to 5 is used and sometimes is followed by a finger snap or some other sound.

Psychoneurosis: Mild mental disorder of a functional type.

Psychosomatic: The interaction (interdependency) of the mental (emotional) and bodily phenomena. Physical symptoms can be the result of our mental/emotional situation. See psychosomatic in the chapter *What Else is Hypnosis?*

Psychosis: Severe mental disorder. This includes things like paranoid schizophrenia and other severe disorders. Normally we do not use hypnosis with these disorders. A clear distinction as to what is reality and what is imagined is needed to successfully apply hypnosis and most psychotics do not demonstrate that.

PTSD: Post traumatic stress disorder. A disorder that is usually associated with a traumatic experience that would be outside the realm of normal human experience such as a murder—especially to someone we are close to—war or other tragic incidents. PTSD can also occur from long term exposure to stresses such as a dysfunctional family life, an abusive family or relationship, etc.

Hypnosis can be a very effective tool for PTSD when used by a skilled professional. Hypnosis was used extensively after WWI and WWII for what was then referred to as shell shock. Dr. Herbert Spiegel, who is well known for his work in hypnosis, was one of the people to use hypnosis for this purpose post war.

Puns: Humor can work well in hypnosis and puns are a method of reframing. One does need to be cautious however when using humor so as not to offend anyone.

Rapid Induction: An induction that takes about three minutes or less.

Rapport: Harmonious accord or relationship. Establishing rapport is very important in hypnosis as well as in other forms of therapy. It is important that we establish a relationship (trust) with our clients. It is important that we don't talk above or insult our client's intelligence. We can also create rapport through our body language. Pierre Janet realized early on the importance of rapport.

Rapport Transfer: A rapport transfer occurs when one operator transfers the hypnosis process to another. Examples: If the hypnotist is working with a client for dental issues the hypnotist will create the proper hypnosis in the office along with a suggestion that when the dentist says or does some (predetermined) trigger the client will immediately be right back in this desirable state of hypnosis. The dentist may or may not be experienced in hypnosis to take advantage of a rapport transfer.

Another type of rapport transfer occurs in a training or research environment where one hypnotist may hand off the trance session to another. This segue helps to prevent any disruption or confusion which could interrupt the subject's session and maintains the rapport created by the first operator.

Read Method: A method of painless childbirth developed by Dr. Grantly Dick Read of England. Dr. Read was not trained in hypnosis and did not believe that he was using hypnosis. However it became very apparent that he was using hypnosis in his process.

Reframing: In hypnosis and NLP redefining, reinterpreting, changing a scene or emotion for a more positive outcome.

Rehearsal Technique (also act as if or pretend method): By acting as though we are in hypnosis, we actually become hypnotized.

Regression: A type of therapy used by skilled hypnotherapists to resolve emotional issues such as but not limited to phobias.

Relaxed Scene Experience: A method of induction whereby taking someone to a relaxed scene creates the desired results, similar to guided imagery. Also see safe place.

REM: Rapid eye movement. REM is characterized by the eyes moving around quickly beneath the eye lids. REM is associated with sleep and dreaming and also with hypnosis, and mainly the theta level of consciousness, though it can also be present in an alpha state. Not the same as eye flutter.

Repressed Memory: Memory that has been held beneath conscious recognition usually due to its traumatic nature. Was first noted by Freud. Often clients are aware of a time in their life where there seems to be a chunk missing. In hypnosis the memory is revivified and healing can take place.

Recently repressed memory has popped up in the area of alien abduction and physical or sexual abuse that did not occur. People can actually experience nightmares, PTSD, etc. from memories that never occurred (Are Recovered Memories Real? By Jill Neimark [Discover Presents The Brain] 2009).

I have had experiences of regressing someone to a time when an alien abduction was thought to have occurred and as much as I would like to uncover some amazing and true experience it has yet to happen. A hypnotist using a leading method of hypnosis might come up with a different result however that would lead to a pseudo regression and would fall into the false memory category.

The memory is not an exact recording of what occurred in the past and some vivid recollections that we might have never occurred at all, yet can evoke the emotions connected with those memories. See also False Memories

Resistance: A factor or factors arising within the client that can make achieving their goal difficult or impossible. Dave Elman said that resistance occurs out of lack of understanding of trance and that by educating the client we will remove the resistance. This is true, but it is unlikely that we could ever remove all of the fear or that we would need to. Confidence on the part of the hypnotist will help alleviate any resistance. Resistance seems to be more prominent for hypnotists who give into its presence (if we expect it to be an issue it probably will be).

Revivification: To revive. In the case of hypnosis revivification comes into play in different ways. Revivification can be an induction; "allow yourself to drift back to the last time that you are sitting in this very recliner, sinking deep into the relaxing sensations of hypnosis, etc." Also, revisiting other past scenes and recreating them for therapeutic or forensic purposes. Point of Reference technique is making use of revivification.

Ritual: Rituals create hypnotic effects (waking hypnosis). See Ceremony and Ritual in the What Else is Hypnosis, chapter of this book.

Rotary Method (Dr. Luy's method): A method of induction that consists of tiring the optic nerve by staring into a series of small rotating mirrors. Groups of people could be quickly hypnotized using this method.

Rule of Three (also compounding): The rule of three states that the first suggestion is weak and the second suggestion has more strength and the third suggestion has optimal strength. When Dave Elman referred to this phenomenon he was saying that the suggestions didn't need to be the same suggestions, but just the giving of suggestions compounded their effect. However we do know that repeating the same or similar suggestion over and over does help to guarantee its acceptance.

Safe Place (AKA special place, happy place, relaxed scene experience, etc.): A hypnotic retreat where we create comfort and safety to de-stress and that we can retreat to for safety

Salpêtrière School: A competing school of thought to the Nancy school, influenced by Charcot. Freud trained primarily with Charcot, but also, Bernhiem, Liebault, Breur and Janet. Charcot believed hypnosis to be a state of hysteria while Bernhiem and Liebault believed hypnosis to be a natural state and of course Bernhiem and Liebault have proved correct.

Sandwich Technique: By layering a negative suggestion between two positive suggestions we create a suggestion sandwich (leverage).

Script: Patter that is delivered from memory or read from a script by the hypnotist to the hypnotized client.

Séance: This term tends to conjure up images of a gypsy woman, in a dimly lit room with candles and a crystal ball, contacting the deceased. Certainly there is some hypnosis being used in that scene. In past history the term "séance" was used to describe the performance of hypnotic experiments in the presence of a few select individuals.

Secondary Gain: A benefit to the client that they would lose by having their issue resolved. For instance: by subconsciously holding on to being overweight the client avoids having sex with an undesirable spouse. Or by having a certain issue the client is able to avoid going to work or doing chores around the house or keeps getting a compensation check.

Self-Hypnosis: Hypnosis performed on oneself without the aid of a facilitator. It is also known as autohypnosis. We say that all formal hypnosis is self-hypnosis since it is only due to the willingness of the subject to be guided by another that allows the process to occur.

Sense Stimulation: Hypnosis can be produced by the stimulation or over-stimulation of the senses. By fixating on any number of types of objects we can tire the eyes so as to cause them to want to relax. Simply by having the client look up at our finger or some other object (pocket watch) we will tire the eyes and cause a desire to relax.

Separating Intention From Behavior: (Erickson) while a habit may be unwanted there may be a perceived benefit such as, "I smoke to relax." So the intention is to relax, which can now be the focus of the session rather than just "not smoking." There are other more beneficial ways to gain relaxation and we can demonstrate this to the client.

Session Intention or Setting the Intention: We can think about the session intention as the goal we wish to achieve. It is important to be clear (between the client and therapist) about exactly what the intention is. It can be easy for the therapist to assume what they believe the intention to be and yet the assumption could be incorrect. Focusing on (repeating) the session intention becomes a suggestion and creates the intention (expectancy) that the result we desire will indeed be the positive outcome that is experienced. See also expectation.

Shamans: The term shaman covers a wide range of tribal healers such as medicine men. Shamans were some of the earliest hypnotists, making use of ceremony, rituals, herbs, potions and incantations to achieve their healings. Witches and witchcraft could easily be included in with the shamans.

Shock: Sudden or violent disturbance in the mental or emotional faculties. When shock occurs (paradigms break down) we are in a hypnotic state, a bypass of the critical faculty has occurred, and we are quite open to suggestion.

SIE: Symptom Intensifying Event Very similar to an SSE (subsequent sensitizing event), however these events occur post SPE (symptom producing event). See also SPE, SSE and ISE.

Sitting (an old term): The voluntary private submission of any person to the hypnotic influence of another.

Skin Picking (Dermatillomania): Obsessive picking at the skin (impulse control disorder). Hypnosis can be very effective with skin picking as with other such issues.

Sleep: A natural periodic suspension of consciousness. While hypnosis and sleep are not necessarily the same thing they are at least close cousins and we can cause hypnotic effects to occur with sleep. Often clients feel that they were asleep; however if we have never been formally hypnotized then sleep is the closest thing that we have to compare it with and so the mind can easily go there. Sleep! Has been the command given be stage hypnotists and early practitioners to gain the state of hypnosis. It is not that sleep is actually what we are trying to achieve, but the word sleep is the word that the mind will accept. If I were to yell hypnosis at someone in order to achieve a trance state it is unlikely that the mind would accept it since there is no model (paradigm) for that term. So sleep works in this case even if it isn't exactly what we want. Also see sleep attached to hypnosis and hypno-sleep.

Sleep Learning: Through recordings a person can learn a foreign language (or other things) while they sleep due to our suggestibility. During WWII this method was widely employed by our armed forces so that soldiers could learn the languages of the countries we were trying to occupy. I had a gentleman come into my office a couple of years ago who had been a bomber pilot during WWII and he said that the pilots memorized their flight plans for the next day by being subjected to audio recordings played while they slept through the night.

Elman capitalized on this phenomenon to do hypnoanalysis on his son to help him with allergies. Elman used a sort of ideomotor signaling and while over a few sessions was not able to complete the analysis the allergic reactions were extremely diminished. Others have been successful with this approach. It would seem that using simple suggestion would be the easiest approach.

I have encouraged clients with children dealing with enuresis (bed wetting) to give their children sleeping suggestions and with good results about half of the time.

Sleep Temples: Also known as dream temples or Egyptian sleep temples. Probably originated with Hindus of ancient India, but were popularized in Egypt, Greece and the Middle East. Many of the treatments given were of a psychological nature through the use of trance and chanting, religious ritual, suggestions of healing, etc. Certainly sleep temples were a very early example of putting the healing effects of hypnosis to work.

Snoring: Snoring made the cut for two reasons: one is that it is something we can use hypnosis to affect, and two, hypnotists often think that snoring means that their client has fallen asleep. This is not necessarily the case at all.

Ask the client; "Are you aware of the sound of my voice?" Most times you will get an affirmative response even though they continue to snore away.

Somatic bridging: See affect bridge.

Somnambulism: Literally translated somnambulism means awake and asleep at the same time. More commonly it has come to mean a deep state of hypnosis. Somnambulism is a great state to give suggestions in and it is the state where painless dentistry and surgery can be performed.

Somnambulist (also natural somnambulist): Someone who enters deep hypnosis easily.

Sounds Patter: See pacing and leading and utilization.

SPE (Symptom Producing Event): An event which causes a breakdown of the normal coping strategies. This is usually when an individual comes in to seek help for their issue.

Special Place: See safe place.

Sports hypnosis: Hypnosis applied to sports performance.

Spontaneous Regression: Occurs when a repressed memory comes to the surface. It could be triggered by something else in the session, and could be a current life experience or a past life.

SSE (Subsequent Sensitizing Event): Events that have the same or similar emotional attachment and that serve to reinforce the ISE (Initial Sensitizing Event). There may be a great number of them. See also ISE.

Stage Hypnosis: Stage hypnosis is the use of hypnosis in front of a group for entertainment purposes. Some of the techniques that have come from stage hypnosis have also proven useful in a clinical setting such as instant inductions.

Stimulus Response: The theory affirms that a response by an organism is directly related to the stimulus preceding it. Relates to conditioned response or Pavlovian response

Stress: A factor that induces emotional and physical tension. Our normal, daily lives (work, relationships, and other changes) all contribute to the stress we experience. Some stress is normal and even desirable; stress can be a motivator, but too much stress can cause serious emotional and physical responses. Hypnosis by its very nature is a great way to deal with stress. Behavioral changes are probably in order for the person who is overly stressed as well.

Stress Reduction: Many methods of stress reduction are common to hypnosis such as guided visualization, relaxed scene experience, point of reference, etc. By its very nature hypnosis is a great tool for stress issues.

Subconscious: The subconscious part of the mind is the imaginative, creative, emotional, habit forming part of the mind. It is where long term or permanent memory is stored. The term subconscious is credited to Pierre Janet. Sometimes subconscious and unconscious are used interchangeably.

Subject: A term sometimes used to describe the person or persons being hypnotized.

Subjective Time: The time the person in hypnosis perceives.

Subliminals: Auditory or visual messages hidden within the context of a larger message. For example, while listening to an audio recording more subtle messages can be hidden (lower volume) within that greater text which the subconscious still picks up on. The effectiveness of subliminal messages is not clear. They may be more effective when the user knows what the hidden messages are which would create an expectation, a kind of indirect suggestion that could have an effect or even a placebo like response for the user.

Substitute Causes: What we would more likely refer to as *reframing* now. Elman referred to substitute causes with disapproval, nowadays this has become a popular and effective method of reframing (*changing personal history* in Ericksonian terminology). In trance a new, more appealing outcome is created in place of the old history, and now the client responds as if this had always been the case.

SUDs Level (subsequent units of distress): A method common to psychotherapy and hypnosis that helps to measure the effectiveness of the work we are doing. A scale of 1-10, with one being no distress to a stimulus, and ten being the most severe amount of distress. Prior to entering into a therapeutic process the SUDs level is tested by subjecting the client to their negative stimulus (could actually put then on an elevator or other stimulus when available, or simply revivify a memory, etc.). After the procedure is complete the client's SUDs level is checked again by subjecting them to that negative stimulus and the SUDs level should have dropped considerably if we were successful.

Suggestibility: How receptive an individual might be to accepting a suggestion. Suggestibility tests help to determine someone's suggestibility.

Suggestibility tests: Simple exercises used to determine a person's ability to receive the hypnotic suggestions.

Suggestion: Suggestion is a common tool used by the hypnotist to achieve the results that are desired. Suggestions can be given as individual statements (affirmations) or as a more extensive length of patter. There are many types of suggestions.

Symptom Substitution: Displacing a symptom to cause it to be more manageable. For instance, moving a pain from one area to a finger tip would make it easier to deal with, and one could see it wouldn't take a lot to eliminate it from there.

Systematic Desensitization: A system typical of cognitive types of therapy, and also applicable to hypnosis, whereby the client is encouraged to face their fears in very small increments until they are finally able to function more normally. Exposure therapy is very similar. Facing our fears is a positive thing to do. The old adage of when you get thrown from a horse you should get right back on, is a good one. If we give into our fears then the horse just keeps getting bigger and bigger until we can never climb on.

In hypnosis we cause this change to occur more quickly by taking the client into their fear and building on those emotions and then taking them back into a safe, comfortable scene that we previously created. Once the unwanted feelings have dissipated we can take them back to the uncomfortable scene and have them experience the feelings associated with that scene, and then return to the safe scene and getting in touch with the comfortable feelings. This sort of ping ponging continues until the unwanted emotions have diminished.

It's generally good to have the client face those situations that they may have been avoiding or felt uncomfortable in before. Once the mind experiences success in these areas it tends to continue on in this positive manner.

Symptom Interrupt or Pattern Interrupt: Most people are familiar with simple pattern or symptom interrupt methods such as having a rubber band around the wrist and whenever we have a thought or a desire toward some unwanted behavior we simply snap the rubber band which not only causes an interruption of that pattern, but also a negative association with it as well.

In hypnosis we can achieve pattern interrupt through the use of confusion, metaphors, embedded suggestions, misdirection, etc.

Theta: Deeper levels of consciousness are experienced at the theta level.

- 4-7 CPS (cycles per second of brainwave activity)
- E.S.P.
- Time distortion
- Suggestibility
- Sleep, including R.E.M.
- Somnambulism
- Painless surgery and dentistry

Time Distortion: A common phenomenon of hypnosis is time distortion. At the end of even a very lengthy hypnosis session the client generally feels he or she was in trance for only a short time (common). Through suggestion we can make the time in trance seem very short or very long.

TMJ (Temporomandibular Joint and Muscle Disorders): Clenching of the jaw, most notably while sleeping (an impulse control disorder). Hypnosis can be very effective for these types of issues.

Trance: Is hypnosis. One definition of trance is hypnosis.

Trance Logic: The logic that occurs in a hypnosis session. Things that seem to make sense while in trance would not make sense in a normal waking state. For instance, in hypnosis I could say to the client, "Notice that there is a large, green giraffe in front of you." In hypnosis this statement makes perfect sense, however if I said the same thing to someone I was sitting next to at the bus stop, they might think I was crazy. This term was probably first applied by Orne who stated that the subject developed a tolerance for logical inconsistencies.

Trance Management: By performing certain tests and by watching for certain clues, we can manage the depth of trance that a client might be in at any given time. This can be particularly important when working with pain, surgery, child birth, etc. There can be a big difference between achieving analgesia and anesthesia.

Trance Residue: After being emerged from hypnosis the subject is still in a state of high suggestibility. This state is often referred to as trance residue.

Transference: Occurs when someone makes someone else the focus of their emotional needs. This usually occurs when a client projects their emotional needs on the therapist. For instance, the client may see the therapist as the parent, friend or lover that they lack in their own life. Some therapies have the therapist acting out the role of that other individual which makes it easy for a client to project onto their therapist. This is less common due to the nature of hypnotherapy, but all hypnotists should be aware because it can cause problems such as a client making the therapist the object of their love (or hate) to the point of stalking, etc. See also Counter Transference.

Trauma: Unusual shock or injury. Could trigger a phobia or other emotional issue.

Traveling Addiction: The belief that the removal of a negative habit in one area will cause another bad habit to arise to take its place. Erickson said that this does not happen and I find that he is correct most of the time.

Trichotillomania: Obsessive pulling of the hair. Pulling may be limited to the scalp, eyelids, eyelashes, pubic hair, other body hair or the pulling may be indiscriminate. Sometimes the loss of hair is hardly noticeable and other times all of the hair may be gone. Eating the hair or biting the roots off may also occur. Often Trichotillomania is combined with skin picking. It is listed as an Impulse Control Disorder in the DSM-IV. Hypnosis can be very effective for this issue.

Triggers: When a state becomes closely associated with a stimulus, that stimulus can later trigger that same state. For instance, when we went to bed at night the act of climbing into the sheets was followed by falling asleep (unconditioned response) so that anytime we climb into the sheets thereafter an expectancy (trigger) has been created so that sleep becomes the normal outcome. This sort of association is created over and over in our lives; just being near or thinking about someone who we have had emotional connection with will bring back (trigger) those emotions to come right back. An old song comes on the radio and triggers the emotions of you dancing with your sweetheart at the Junior Prom.

As hypnotists we create and use these anchors and triggers to our best advantage. Even the recliner becomes a trigger. Because the client has sat in that recliner before and became very relaxed, the expectation (trigger) occurs that this is what naturally happens. The hypnotist can take advantage of this by bringing the client's attention to the sensations or to the recliner and the sensations of relaxation (utilization), and create an induction or other useful sensations. We can anchor feelings in trance that we can trigger at a later time to use to our advantage (see kinesthetic anchors [also the chapter on conditioned response in this book]).

Truisms: A suggestion that by its very nature is so likely and so believable that it is easily accepted by the subconscious mind.

Uptime Trance: There are two types of trance that can be occurring simultaneously during a hypnosis session. The therapist is in what is called uptime trance. This means that the therapist is also in a hypnotic trance, but only to a level to which he or she can still perform all of the functions necessary. Not all hypnotists go into uptime trance; some will stay very analytical and consciously focused. Uptime trance is considered to be a positive phenomenon.

Unconscious: The unconscious, for our purposes, is the part of the mind that has to do with the autonomic nervous system, bodily functions, and the nervous system. Unconscious and subconscious are sometimes used interchangeably.

Under Hypnosis: This is a term that is all too commonly used by lay people, as well as some hypnotists, that should not be applied to hypnosis. The client is not being put under anything and the hypnotist does not put anyone under. I think the underlying message is that someone will be under the hypnotist's control or spell (or as if we were under the influence of a drug) and this is not the case. We are entering a state of hypnosis or going into a state of hypnosis and not under anything.

Utilization: Making use in hypnosis of what is obvious in the client's world. This term has come to mean different things. When Milton Erickson popularized the use of this term he seemed to be referring more to using objects and events that would be known to occur in a client's environment to help trigger positive results—sort of a posthypnotic suggestion. An example would be: *Passing by the old school house near the meadow, or stopping at the Piggly Wiggly is much like when you were with your children* (evoking certain feelings and changes). There could be many of these utilization experiences presented in a trance.

Utilization has become popularized to incorporate the environmental things that might become disruptive in a clients session so as to remove them as a possible distraction. Such as *The sounds of the road crew outside only serves to take you deeper.* See also sounds patter and pacing and leading which are methods of utilization.

Voodoo: Is probably a nocebo effect more than anything. If we believe (expectation) that a spell has been placed on us we may respond in the intended way.

Waking Hypnosis: Hypnotic results can be achieved in a waking state. There is an entire chapter in this book devoted to waking hypnosis.

Waking Suggestion: Waking suggestions are those suggestions given in a normal state of conscious which achieve hypnotic results. See the chapter on waking hypnosis.

Womb Experience: Through regression therapy, many causes for anxiety or phobias are traced back to the time prior to the client's birth when he or she was in the womb.

Witchcraft: True witchcraft is really the application of folk lore and folk remedies. Some of these remedies include herbs and potions, but also various rituals which include things like candle burning, burning of symbols, forming sacred circles, chanting, incantations, etc. It would not be a stretch to put witches in with shamans. Certainly we can see that hypnosis is part of the witchcraft tradition.

Yes Momentum: See pacing and leading.

Yes Set: See pacing and leading.

REFERENCE RESOURCES AND
RECOMMENDED READING

Many of the books that I use for reference are old and out of print. Many of these books can be found in used bookstores or online. I love going into a used bookstore and finding some dusty, old book on hypnosis. Some of the old books you find can just be laughable, talking about controlling people's minds and such, but lots of others have wonderful and pertinent information that we can put to use. Keep in mind the era in which some of these books were written, and what current paradigms were at that time, and know that we have learned things that would make some of that information irrelevant at this time.

Sigmund Freud had some beliefs about hypnosis that we know to be totally inaccurate now. Had he not held to some of these mis-beliefs about hypnosis and continued to use it as his method of psychotherapy the world of hypnosis and its use would likely be much different now. It's amazing to me how long this journey of hypnosis has been going on and what some of those ground breaking pioneers were able to accomplish.

The Rev. C. Scot Giles, D.Min, BCC, DNGH
   With Arthur A. Leidecker, BCH, CI
   Complementary Medical Hypnotism Certification
   National Guild of Hypnotists

The National Guild of Hypnosis (NGH)
   Merrimac, NH
   www.ngh.net

General Techniques of Hypnotism
André M. Wietzenhoffer
1957 Grune & Stratton, Inc.

Hypnotism
Axel Wayne Bacon
1945 Nelson Hall Co.
Hypnotherapy
Dave Elman
1964
This classic book is still quite available through Westwood Publishing Co. and should be in every hypnotist's library.

Advanced Techniques of Hypnosis
Melvin Powers
1953 Wilshire Book Co.

Self Hypnosis
Melvin Powers
1956 Wilshire Book Co.

Hypnotism Revealed
Melvin Powers
1949 Wilshire Book Co.

The Complete Guide to Hypnosis
Leslie Le Cron
1971 Barnes & Knoble

Gerald F. Kein
Omni Hypnosis
830 North Woodland Blvd
Deland Florida 32720
Trainings, videos and literature available
www.omnihypnosis.com

Modern Hypnosis
Edited and Compiled by
Lesley Kuhn and
Salvatore Russo, Ph.D
Many contributors including Erickson
1947 Psychological Library Publishers

Hypnosis In The Relief Of Pain
Hilgard and Hilgard
1975 William Kaufman Inc.
What Is Hypnosis
Andrew Salter
1941 The Noonday Press

The Power of the Past
Drake Eastburn
2007 Trafford Publishing

Power Patter
Drake Eastburn
2007 Eastburn

No Time to Waist—Powerful Hypnosis Weight Loss Secrets
Drake Eastburn
2010 D. James Publishing

The Power of Suggestion
Drake Eastburn
2010 Trafford Publishing

It's Conceivable! Hypnosis for Fertility
Lynsi Eastburn
2006 Trafford Publishing

HypnoVision
Lisette Scholl
1997 Westwood Publishing

New Master Course in Hypnotism
>Harry Arons
>1948 Power Publishers

Experimental Hypnosis
>Leslie M. LeCron and many contributors
>1948 The Macmillan Co.
>*I have referenced this book many times and contributions to this book were made by some of the biggest names in hypnosis including Milton Erickson, Wietzenhoffer, Watson, Le Cron and others. If you come across a copy of this book I would suggest you grab it up. There is some wonderful insight into the world of hypnosis as we now know it.*

Trancework
>Michael D. Yapko
>1990 Brunner/Mazel, Inc.
>*Readily available and highly recommended. This is one of the most complete and modern treatises on modern clinical hypnosis that can be found. Yapko has other worthwhile books as well.*

The Journals of Lewis and Clark
>Bernard DeVoto
>Houghton Mifflin Co.

The Silva Method
>*Google them and you will find an extensive website of information.*

Trance and Treatment
>Drs. Herbert and David Spiegel
>1978 American Psychiatric Press
>*This book contains the use of the eye method of determining hypnotizability.*

From Mesmer to Freud
>Adam Crabtree
>1993 Yale University Press

The Gestalt Institute of the Rockies
Golden, Co. 80401
303-426-8211
303-985-3534

Analytical Hypnotherapy/Principles and Practices
E.A. Barnett, MD
1989 Westwood Publishing

Modern Hypnosis
Masud Ansari, PhD
Mas-Press 1982

Franz Anton Mesmer- Between God and Devil
James Wycoff
1975 Prentice-Hall
A gem if you can find it. This book really gives insight into early modern hypnosis and a good look into the world at the time of Mesmer and into those who influenced him and who he influenced.

Unleashing Your Brilliance
Brian E. Walsh, PhD
2005 Walsh
Walsh Seminars Ltd.
Box 963, Victoria, BC V8W 2R9 Canada
www.UnleashingBook.com
Highly recommended.

Hypnotherapeutic Techniques
The Practice of Clinical Hypnosis Volume I
John G. Watkins, PhD
1986 Irvington Publishers Inc.

Animal Hypnosis
Dr. F. A. Volgyesi
1963 Willshire Book Co.
Translated from earlier German publishing.

Practical Lessons in Hypnotism
        WM. Wesley Cook, A.M., M.D.
        1943 Willey Book Co. (This is the reprint date and there was no original
        copyright date in the book, but my guess is that it is quite old.)

The Experience of Hypnosis
        Ernest R. Hilgard
        1965 Harbinger
        How To Practice Suggestion And Autosuggestion
        Emile Coué
        1992 Sun Publishing Company
        Originally Published by American Library Services 1923

My Method
        Emile Coué
        1923 Doubleday Page and Company
        1999 Arthur A. Leidecker
        The Leidecker Institute
        Schaumberg, Illinois 60195
        artsprivatemail@aol.com

About the Author

Drake Eastburn is a Board Certified Hypnotherapist and Certified Hypnotherapy Instructor through the National Guild of Hypnotists (NGH). He has worked in the field of hypnotism for more than three decades and maintains a thriving private practice with three Denver-area locations. Drake and his wife, Lynsi, also run a professional hypnosis training facility *Eastburn Institute of Hypnosis* and have trained therapists worldwide.

Drake is the author of six books on the subject of hypnotism. He is an avid reader of anything and everything in the areas of genetics and neuropsychology.

Drake lives in the Denver area (Colorado) with his wife, Lynsi, sons Kelly Brûlé and Dylan Brûlé, and two dogs Boo Radley and Scout.

Also Available from Eastburn Hypnotherapy Center

- Hypnotherapy Certification Training
- Hypnotherapy Advanced Training Courses
- Hypnotherapy DVD Training:
  - Body Focused Repetitive Behaviors
  - Sleep
  - Transformational Replay (Regression)
  - Puffed Enuff™ (Smoking Cessation)
  - No Time to Waist Hypnosis Weight Loss Training

Specialty Recordings by Drake Eastburn:

- Weight Mastery for Youth—Daytime & Nighttime CDs
- Prosperity—Daytime & Nighttime CDs
- Lift Your Spirits—Affirmations & Afformations CDs
- Nighttime Healing CD
- Stress Reduction CD
- Sports Enhancement/Endurance CDs

Books by Drake Eastburn:

- Power of the Past
- Power Patter
- No Time to Waist—Powerful Hypnosis Weight Loss Secrets You Need to Know
- The Power of Suggestion

Specialty Recordings by Lynsi Eastburn:

- HypnoFertility* CD
- IVF Assistant—4 CD Package
- Natural Fertility—4 CD Package
- Infinity of Wellness: Hypnosis/Aromatherapy Kits

Books by Lynsi Eastburn:

- It's Conceivable! *Hypnosis for Fertility*

And Much More . . . For more information about
Eastburn Hypnotherapy Center please contact us:

www.hypnodenver.com ~ 303-424-2331

LaVergne, TN USA
22 February 2011
217581LV00002B/172/P